SARDINIA
TRAVEL GUIDE 2025

By

Cathy Dawson

COPYRIGHT

All rights reserved. No part of this publication may be reproduced, distributed, or transmitted in any form or by any means, including photocopying, recording or other electronic or mechanical methods, without the prior written permission of the publisher, except in the case of brief quotation embodied in critical reviews and certain other noncommercial uses permitted by copyright law.

Copyright by Cathy Dawson 2025

CONTENTS

INTRODUCTION 5
    WHY VISIT SARDINIA 5
    HOW TO USE THIS GUIDE 8
    PERSONAL REFLECTION FROM AUTHOR 13

CHAPTER 1: PLANNIG YOUR TRIP 16
    TRAVEL REQUIREMENTS 16
    WHEN TO VISIT 20
    TRAVEL INSURANCE INFORMATIONS 24
    PACKING GUIDE 29
    HEALTH & SAFETY TIPS 34
    COMMON SARDINIAN PHRASES 39

CHAPTER 2: GETTING TO AND AROUND SARDINIA 43
    ARRIVING BY AIR 43
    FERRIES TRAVEL 48
    TAXIS 53
    PUBLIC TRANSIT 57
    CAR RENTAL 62

CHAPTER 3: MUST-VISIT DESTINATIONS 67
    COSTA SMERALDA 67
    LA MADDALENA 72
    OGLIASTRA 77
    CAGLIARI: THE ISLAND'S CAPITAL 82
    ALGHERO 87
    ORISTANO 93
    OLBIA 98

CHAPTER 4: ATTRACTIONS 104
    ANCIENT NURAGHE SITES: BARUMINI & MORE 104
    SPECTACULAR BEACHES: SPIAGGIA DELLA PELOSA, CALA LUNA & COSTA REI . 109
    NATURAL WONDERS: GOLA DI GORROPU & MONTE ARCOSU 114

LANDMARKS: ROMAN AMPHITHEATERS, CATHEDRALS & TOWERS 118

CHAPTER 5: ACCOMMODATION 124

HOTELS & RESORTS 124
BUDGET STAYS & CAMPING 129
CHARMING B&BS & AGRITURISMI STAYS 134

CHAPTER 6: CUISINE AND DINING 139

MUST-TRY SARDINIAN DISHES 139
FRESH SEAFOOD & COASTAL CUISINE 143
SWEETS & DESSERTS 147
WINES AND SPIRITS 151
EXPLORING LOCAL MARKETS 155

CHAPTER 7: OUTDOOR ADVENTURES 161

HIKING & TREKKING 161
WATER SPORTS & COASTAL ACTIVITIES 166
CLIMBING & CAVING 170
WILDLIFE ENCOUNTERS 175

CONCLUSION: PRACTICAL TIPS & TRAVEL ITINERARIES 180

MONEY MATTERS: CURRENCY, BANKING & BUDGETING 180
ONE-WEEK ITINERARY 185
TWO-WEEK ITINERARY 190

INTRODUCTION

Why Visit Sardinia

Sardinia is one of those places that leaves a lasting impression—a destination that, once visited, lingers in your heart and mind long after you've returned home. It's a land of remarkable contrasts, where ancient history meets natural beauty, and vibrant cultures blend seamlessly with untouched landscapes. Why visit Sardinia? The question is almost difficult to answer in a few words, because there are so many reasons to make this Mediterranean island a must-visit. For those who are drawn to destinations that offer both relaxation and adventure, rich culture and breathtaking landscapes, Sardinia delivers on all fronts.

One of the first things that draw visitors to Sardinia is its stunning coastline, which is among the most beautiful in the Mediterranean. The island is surrounded by crystal-clear waters, with some of the most pristine beaches you'll ever lay eyes on. Picture yourself walking barefoot on white sand, with the turquoise sea stretching endlessly before you. Beaches like **Spiaggia della Pelosa**, **Cala Luna**, and **Costa Rei** are not just postcard-perfect, they're places where you can truly unwind, enjoy the sun, or partake in water activities like snorkeling, swimming, or even windsurfing. Each beach is unique in its own right, offering something different depending on your mood, from secluded coves to lively spots where you can enjoy beachside cafes. If you're someone who enjoys the ocean, Sardinia's coastlines will undoubtedly captivate you.

But Sardinia isn't just about beaches. This island is home to **some of the most unspoiled and diverse landscapes in Europe**. From the towering cliffs and lush valleys of the inland to the rugged peaks of the **Gennargentu Mountains**, Sardinia offers a wide range of outdoor experiences for every type of traveler. Whether you're a hiker, a mountain biker, or someone who enjoys simply immersing yourself in nature, Sardinia has something for you. Take a hike through the **Gola di Gorropu Canyon**, one of the deepest canyons in Europe, or explore the serene **Monte Arcosu Reserve**, which is home to native wildlife. These natural wonders are the perfect antidote to the stresses of modern life, providing tranquility, adventure, and a deep connection to the land.

For history lovers, Sardinia is a treasure trove of ancient sites and ruins. The island has been home to several civilizations, from the **Nuragic people**—whose mysterious stone structures, known as nuraghes, dot the landscape—to the Romans and Catalans. Exploring Sardinia's ancient past is like stepping into a living museum. Sites like **Barumini**, with its complex of nuraghes, offer a glimpse into a prehistoric culture that's over 3,000 years old. Sardinia's towns and cities are also steeped in history, from the **Roman amphitheater** in Cagliari to the **medieval architecture** of Alghero. You'll feel the weight of history wherever you go, making every step a journey through time.

In addition to its natural and historical appeal, Sardinia also offers a rich cultural experience. The island has its own unique traditions, from **folk music and dance** to the famous **Cavalcata Sarda** festival in Sassari, where locals celebrate their heritage with processions, music, and vibrant costumes. The **Sardinian language**—a blend of Latin and other influences—is still spoken in many villages, giving visitors a true sense of the island's ancient roots. Sardinia's culinary traditions are another strong draw, with dishes that highlight the island's connection to the land and sea. Whether you're savoring **porceddu** (roast suckling pig), indulging in freshly caught seafood, or enjoying the island's famous cheeses and wines, Sardinia's food is a true reflection of its culture and history.

What makes Sardinia particularly special is the sense of **authenticity** it offers. While some Mediterranean destinations have become heavily commercialized, Sardinia retains much of its charm and character. The island's villages are picturesque and often feel untouched by modern development, with narrow streets, stone houses, and tranquil squares that invite exploration. And despite being a popular tourist destination, Sardinia never feels overcrowded. There's always a quiet corner to retreat to, whether it's a secluded beach, a mountain trail, or a quiet café in a charming town.

For those seeking an escape from the ordinary, Sardinia offers an experience that is both relaxing and enriching. It's a place where you can unwind in the beauty of nature, dive deep into its rich history, or simply enjoy the pleasures of authentic island life. Sardinia isn't just a place to visit—it's a place that stays with you, urging you to return time and again. Whether you're a beach lover, an adventure seeker, a history enthusiast, or someone who simply wants to experience the best of Mediterranean life, Sardinia promises to be a destination that will exceed your expectations.

How to Use This Guide

This guide is designed to be your ultimate companion for exploring Sardinia, providing all the essential information you need to plan your trip, navigate the island, and make the most of your time in this Mediterranean paradise. Whether you are visiting for a weekend getaway, a week-long adventure, or an extended stay, this guide is structured to give you both a comprehensive overview and in-depth details about Sardinia's best attractions, cultural experiences, and practical travel tips. The goal is to make your journey as smooth and enjoyable as possible, offering insights from a traveler's perspective, local recommendations, and firsthand experiences.

This guide is divided into several sections, each covering a different aspect of your Sardinian adventure. It starts with an introduction to Sardinia, giving you a sense of what makes this island special and why it should be on your travel list. The next sections provide all the essential pre-trip planning details, including visa requirements, the best time to visit, health and safety tips, and practical advice such as currency, language, and customs. These sections will help you prepare for your journey and ensure you arrive well-informed and ready to explore. Packing recommendations, transportation options, and local etiquette are also covered, helping you avoid common travel pitfalls and maximize your experience.

Once you arrive, navigating Sardinia efficiently will be crucial to making the most of your time. The guide explains the various transportation options available, from renting a car, which is highly recommended for accessing Sardinia's hidden gems, to using public buses and trains, which are more suited for travel between larger towns and cities. It also includes tips for driving in Sardinia, understanding local road signs, and using ferries to reach smaller islands and coastal areas. Knowing how to get around is key to ensuring you don't miss out on some of the island's most spectacular locations, especially those that are off the beaten path.

For those looking to explore Sardinia by region, this guide breaks the island down into its distinct areas, highlighting the must-see attractions, cultural landmarks, and natural wonders of each. The northern part of the island is known for its glamorous Costa Smeralda, the stunning archipelago of La Maddalena, and picturesque towns like Alghero, which blends Catalan influences with Sardinian traditions. The east coast offers dramatic cliffs, turquoise waters, and hidden beaches like Cala Luna and Cala Goloritzé, accessible only by boat or a scenic hike. The west is home to charming towns like Bosa, historic sites like Tharros, and vast beaches ideal for windsurfing and outdoor adventures. The south, anchored by the vibrant capital city of Cagliari, showcases a mix of history, nightlife, and some of the island's best beaches, while the rugged interior of Sardinia offers a chance to experience authentic village life, stunning landscapes, and archaeological treasures.

To help you choose the right activities, this guide offers detailed insights into Sardinia's top experiences, including historical sites, outdoor adventures, food and wine experiences, and cultural traditions. Whether you are interested in visiting the ancient Nuragic ruins, hiking in the Gennargentu mountains, exploring the stunning coastline by boat, or indulging in traditional Sardinian cuisine, this guide provides recommendations on what to see and do based on different interests and travel styles. It also includes information on activity costs, booking recommendations, and tips for avoiding tourist traps, ensuring that you get the best value and experience during your visit.

Accommodation is another key consideration when planning a trip, and this guide provides an overview of Sardinia's lodging options, from luxury resorts along the Costa Smeralda to budget-friendly agriturismi in the countryside, boutique hotels in charming towns, and unique stays like historic mansions or seaside villas. Each type of accommodation offers a different perspective on Sardinia, and this guide helps you choose based on location, budget, and the type of experience you are looking for, whether it's a relaxing retreat, an active adventure, or an immersive cultural stay.

Food is a major highlight of any trip to Sardinia, and this guide includes an extensive section on the island's culinary traditions, signature dishes, and dining recommendations. Sardinian cuisine is distinct from mainland Italian food, with influences from its pastoral heritage and Mediterranean surroundings. From savoring the famous suckling pig known as porceddu to tasting handmade pasta like culurgiones, and from enjoying fresh seafood to sampling local cheeses and wines, this guide will help you discover the best places to eat, from high-end restaurants to traditional trattorias and street food vendors. It also covers local dining customs, tipping etiquette, and must-try dishes to ensure that you fully enjoy Sardinia's gastronomic delights.

To make your itinerary planning easier, this guide includes suggested travel itineraries based on different lengths of stay and travel preferences. Whether you have three days, a week, or more, the itineraries provide a balanced mix of cultural exploration, beach time, outdoor activities, and relaxation, ensuring that you experience the best of Sardinia without feeling rushed. Itineraries are also tailored to different types of travelers, from families with children to adventure seekers, couples looking for a romantic escape, and history enthusiasts eager to uncover Sardinia's past.

In addition to practical travel tips, this guide includes insider recommendations on how to experience Sardinia beyond the typical tourist attractions. Suggestions for off-the-beaten-path locations, local markets, traditional festivals, and hidden beaches allow travelers to discover the authentic side of Sardinia. It also provides advice on how to interact with locals, understand Sardinian customs, and participate in cultural experiences such as cheese-making, wine tasting, or attending a traditional festival.

For those who like to travel sustainably, this guide includes tips on eco-friendly travel, responsible tourism, and ways to minimize your environmental impact while exploring Sardinia. Whether it's choosing locally owned accommodations, supporting small businesses, or respecting nature reserves, this guide offers advice on how to enjoy the island responsibly while preserving its beauty for future generations.

Throughout this guide, you'll also find essential information on emergency contacts, health services, and important numbers in case you need assistance during your trip. Information on local pharmacies, hospitals, and travel insurance considerations ensures that you are prepared for any situation while traveling in Sardinia.

Ultimately, this guide is designed to be your go-to resource before and during your trip, providing all the information you need in a well-organized, easy-to-use format. Whether you prefer to plan every detail in advance or like to explore spontaneously, this guide allows you to navigate Sardinia with confidence and ease. It combines practical advice with local insights, ensuring that your experience is not only smooth but also enriched with meaningful connections and unforgettable moments. Sardinia is an island that rewards curiosity, and with this guide, you will have everything you need to immerse yourself in its breathtaking landscapes, fascinating history, delicious food, and welcoming culture. No matter your travel style or interests, this guide ensures that you make the most of your time in Sardinia, turning your journey into an extraordinary adventure filled with lasting memories.

Personal Reflection from Author

Sardinia has always felt like a place where time slows down, where the rhythm of life follows the tides and the wind that sweeps across its rugged landscapes. As I wandered through its ancient villages, sun-drenched coastlines, and mountainous interiors, I felt a deep connection to this island—one that I hope to share with you through this guide. Writing this book has been more than just documenting places to visit; it has been a personal journey of discovery, an opportunity to understand Sardinia's heart and soul beyond its stunning scenery.

I remember my first visit vividly—the scent of myrtle in the air, the warmth of the Mediterranean sun on my skin, and the sound of waves gently lapping against the rocky shores. Sardinia immediately felt different from other destinations. It wasn't just the natural beauty that captivated me, but also the **authenticity of its people**, the **rich history embedded in its stones**, and the **sense of pride Sardinians have for their land**. It didn't take long before I realized that this island is more than just a summer escape—it is a world of its own, shaped by traditions, ancient legacies, and an unbreakable bond with nature.

As a traveler, I have always sought out destinations that offer more than postcard-perfect scenery. I look for places where stories unfold in everyday life, where the past is alive in the present, and where there is something to be learned from every encounter. Sardinia is exactly that kind of place. It is a land of contrasts—wild yet welcoming, ancient yet timeless. Here, you can find **nuraghe ruins older than the pyramids of Egypt**, medieval cities steeped in history, and untouched natural landscapes that have remained the same for centuries.

One of the most striking things about Sardinia is its diversity. The coastline is lined with some of the most breathtaking beaches in the world, yet venture inland, and you'll find a completely different side of the island—rolling hills, dense forests, and remote villages where time seems to stand still. I was drawn to the island's **pastoral traditions**, to the shepherds who still produce cheese using age-old methods, to the **hidden hiking trails** that lead to spectacular vistas, and to the **locals who welcome you with open arms**, eager to share their culture and way of life. Sardinia taught me that travel isn't just about sightseeing—it's about experiencing a place through its people, its flavors, its history, and its rhythm of life.

Writing this guide was a way for me to bring together all of those experiences and insights, ensuring that visitors can truly appreciate **what makes Sardinia special**. I wanted to go beyond the usual tourist recommendations and offer **a deeper, more personal perspective**—one that captures the essence of Sardinia as a place that is both captivating and deeply rooted in its traditions. Whether you are here for a few days or planning an extended stay, I hope this book helps you explore Sardinia not just as a visitor, but as someone who wishes to connect with its soul. My greatest hope is that as you set foot on this extraordinary island, you will feel the same sense of wonder and appreciation that I did—and that Sardinia will leave an imprint on you, just as it did on me.

CHAPTER 1: PLANNIG YOUR TRIP

Travel Requirements

Traveling to Sardinia requires careful preparation, and understanding passport and visa requirements is one of the most important steps to ensure a smooth journey. As an autonomous region of Italy, Sardinia follows the same entry regulations as the rest of the country, which means that travelers must comply with Italian immigration policies when planning their visit. The specific requirements depend on your nationality, the duration of your stay, and the purpose of your visit, so it is crucial to check the latest regulations well in advance to avoid any last-minute complications.

For citizens of the European Union (EU) and Schengen Area countries, entering Sardinia is straightforward. These travelers do not need a visa and can enter the island using a valid national identity card or passport. There are no border checks when arriving from another Schengen country, making travel seamless for EU visitors. However, it is always recommended to carry a valid passport or ID card, as airlines and ferry operators may require identification before boarding, and some accommodation providers may request a copy of your documents at check-in. If traveling from an EU country, there is also no limit on the length of stay, allowing visitors to explore Sardinia at their leisure without the need for additional paperwork.

For non-EU travelers, visa requirements vary depending on nationality. Citizens of the United States, Canada, the United Kingdom, Australia, New Zealand, and several other countries can enter Sardinia visa-free for short stays of up to 90 days within a 180-day period under the Schengen Visa Waiver Program. This applies to tourism, business, or family visits but does not permit employment or long-term residency. Travelers from these countries must ensure that their passport is valid for at least three months beyond their intended departure date from the Schengen Area. While visa-free entry allows flexible travel within Italy and other Schengen countries, it is important to track the number of days spent in the region, as overstaying the 90-day limit could lead to fines, deportation, or future entry bans.

For those who require a visa to enter Italy, the Schengen Visa is the standard option. This visa must be obtained before departure from an Italian consulate or embassy in the traveler's home country. The application process generally requires submitting a completed form, a valid passport with at least two blank pages, passport-sized photographs, proof of travel arrangements such as flight tickets and accommodation bookings, travel insurance covering medical expenses, and proof of sufficient financial means to support the stay. Processing times vary, but it is advisable to apply at least a month in advance to allow for any delays. The standard Schengen Visa allows travel within the entire Schengen Area for up to 90 days within a 180-day period, making it ideal for those who plan to visit Sardinia as part of a larger European itinerary.

For travelers planning to stay in Sardinia for more than 90 days, a long-term visa or residence permit is required. This applies to individuals moving to the island for work, study, or extended stays with family. The process for obtaining a long-term visa is more complex and often requires additional documentation, such as a work contract, university acceptance letter, or proof of family ties. Once in Italy, long-term visa holders must apply for a residence permit (permesso di soggiorno) within eight days of arrival at the local police headquarters (Questura). It is crucial to start this process promptly to avoid any legal issues during the stay.

Regardless of visa requirements, all travelers should be prepared for routine border checks, especially when arriving by air or sea. Immigration officers may ask for proof of onward travel, accommodation details, or evidence of sufficient funds to cover expenses. Although these checks are not always conducted, it is best to have all necessary documents readily available to prevent any inconvenience. Travelers from visa-exempt countries should also be aware that the European Union is introducing the European Travel Information and Authorization System (ETIAS), which is expected to come into effect soon. This will require visa-exempt visitors to complete an online authorization before traveling to the Schengen Area, including Sardinia. The process will involve a security screening and a small fee, but once approved, ETIAS authorization will be valid for multiple entries over several years.

For those traveling with children, additional documentation may be required depending on the country of origin. Some nations require minors traveling with only one parent or guardian to carry a notarized letter of consent from the absent parent, while others may request birth certificates or other proof of relationship. It is advisable to check with the relevant authorities to ensure compliance with travel regulations for minors.

In addition to passport and visa considerations, travelers should also be aware of customs regulations when entering Sardinia. Visitors arriving from outside the EU must comply with duty-free allowances on goods such as alcohol, tobacco, and luxury items. It is important to declare any restricted or high-value items to avoid potential fines or confiscation. Those carrying prescription medications should bring a copy of their prescription and ensure that the medication is legally permitted in Italy. For travelers bringing pets, EU regulations require microchipping, a valid pet passport, and up-to-date rabies vaccinations, with additional requirements for animals arriving from non-EU countries.

To ensure a hassle-free experience, it is recommended to make copies of all important travel documents, including passports, visas, insurance policies, and emergency contact details. Keeping both physical and digital copies in a secure location can be invaluable in case of loss or theft. Additionally, registering with your country's embassy or consulate in Italy can provide extra security and assistance in emergencies, such as lost passports or unexpected travel disruptions.

Understanding passport and visa requirements is an essential part of planning a trip to Sardinia, and staying informed about current regulations will help avoid any unnecessary travel complications. By ensuring that all necessary documents are prepared in advance, visitors can focus on enjoying Sardinia's breathtaking landscapes, rich history, and vibrant culture without worrying about entry restrictions. Whether visiting for a short holiday, an extended stay, or a business trip, having the correct travel documentation is the first step toward a smooth and memorable experience on this enchanting island.

When to Visit

Deciding when to visit Sardinia depends largely on personal preferences, as the island offers something unique in every season. With its Mediterranean climate, Sardinia enjoys hot, dry summers and mild, wet winters, making it a year-round destination for different types of travelers. Understanding the seasonal variations in weather, tourist activity, and available experiences can help visitors plan their trip to make the most of their time on the island. Each season offers its own charm, and while summer is the most popular time for beachgoers, spring and autumn provide perfect conditions for outdoor adventures, while winter offers a quieter, more cultural experience.

Summer is the peak tourist season in Sardinia, attracting visitors with its warm temperatures, sunny skies, and idyllic beaches. From June through September, the island's coastal areas are bustling with activity as travelers from around the world flock to famous beaches like Costa Smeralda, Cala Mariolu, and La Pelosa. Average temperatures during the summer months range between 25°C and 35°C (77°F to 95°F), with some inland areas reaching even higher temperatures. The sea is at its warmest, making it perfect for swimming, snorkeling, and diving. While the beaches and resort towns are lively, this is also the most expensive time to visit, with accommodation prices at their highest and popular tourist spots crowded with visitors. Those planning to visit during summer should book accommodations well in advance and be prepared for higher costs, especially in sought-after locations. The warm evenings allow for vibrant nightlife, with beach clubs, open-air concerts, and traditional festivals creating a lively atmosphere across the island. Despite the crowds, summer remains the best time for those looking to experience Sardinia's famous coastline and enjoy a true Mediterranean holiday.

Spring is one of the best times to visit Sardinia, offering a pleasant climate, fewer tourists, and stunning natural landscapes. From March to May, the island comes to life with blooming wildflowers, green hills, and comfortable temperatures ranging from 15°C to 25°C (59°F to 77°F). This is an excellent season for outdoor activities such as hiking in the Supramonte mountains, exploring the Gennargentu National Park, or taking scenic drives through the countryside. The mild temperatures make sightseeing enjoyable without the intense heat of summer, allowing visitors to explore historic sites, archaeological ruins, and charming villages at a relaxed pace. Spring is also a great time for cycling enthusiasts, as the roads are less crowded and the weather is ideal for long rides through Sardinia's diverse landscapes. The beaches remain relatively quiet during this time, though the sea can still be a bit cool for swimming, especially in March and early April. However, by late May, the water begins to warm up, and visitors can enjoy peaceful shorelines before the summer crowds arrive. Spring is also a fantastic time to experience Sardinia's traditional festivals, such as the Sant'Efisio procession in Cagliari, one of the most important religious celebrations in the region.

Autumn, from September to November, is another ideal time to visit Sardinia, offering warm temperatures, fewer tourists, and a relaxed atmosphere. September, in particular, is a perfect month for those who enjoy beach vacations but prefer to avoid the peak season crowds. The sea remains warm from the summer heat, making it an excellent time for swimming and water sports. By October, the island begins to transition into a quieter season, with mild temperatures ranging from 18°C to 28°C (64°F to 82°F), making it an excellent time for hiking, wine tasting, and exploring Sardinia's cultural sites. Autumn is also the season for food festivals, with events celebrating local delicacies such as chestnuts, mushrooms, and truffles. The vineyards are in full harvest mode, making it an excellent time to visit wineries and sample Sardinia's famous Cannonau and Vermentino wines. Prices for accommodations and flights begin to drop after the busy summer season, making it an affordable time to visit while still enjoying pleasant weather. While the chances of rain increase in November, particularly in the mountainous regions, coastal areas often remain sunny and enjoyable. This is an excellent season for those who appreciate a slower pace and a more immersive experience in Sardinia's local culture and natural beauty.

Winter in Sardinia, from December to February, is the island's quietest season, with fewer tourists and a more laid-back atmosphere. While the coastal towns experience cooler temperatures ranging from 10°C to 16°C (50°F to 61°F), the mountain areas can be significantly colder, with occasional snowfall in the higher elevations of the Gennargentu mountains. Although beach activities are less appealing during winter, this season is perfect for exploring the island's historical and cultural sites without the crowds. Cities like Cagliari, Alghero, and Sassari remain lively, offering a glimpse into Sardinian daily life with bustling markets, cozy cafés, and traditional cuisine. Winter is also an excellent time for travelers interested in local traditions, as many of the island's most unique festivals take place during this period, including the Mamuthones and Issohadores carnival in the town of Mamoiada, where ancient masked figures perform ritual dances. While some coastal resorts and tourist services close for the season, visitors can still enjoy Sardinia's natural beauty, taking advantage of lower accommodation prices and a peaceful atmosphere. Those interested in experiencing the island's culinary delights can indulge in hearty winter dishes such as lamb stew, malloreddus pasta, and local cheeses while enjoying the warmth of traditional agriturismo hospitality.

Regardless of the season, Sardinia offers a diverse range of experiences that cater to all types of travelers. Those seeking a classic beach vacation will find summer to be the best time to visit, while spring and autumn provide ideal conditions for active travelers looking to explore the island's landscapes and cultural heritage. Winter may not be the most popular season, but it offers a unique and authentic experience for those looking to discover Sardinia beyond its summer beaches. No matter when you choose to visit, Sardinia's charm, natural beauty, and rich history ensure a memorable journey filled with unforgettable moments. Proper planning and understanding the seasonal differences will allow travelers to tailor their trip to match their interests, ensuring the best possible experience on this stunning Mediterranean island.

Travel Insurance Informations

Travel insurance is an essential consideration for anyone planning a trip to Sardinia, providing financial protection and peace of mind in case of unexpected events. Whether visiting for a short vacation, an extended stay, or an adventure-filled getaway, having the right insurance coverage can help mitigate risks related to medical emergencies, trip cancellations, lost baggage, or other unforeseen situations that could disrupt your travel plans. While Sardinia is generally a safe and well-developed destination, accidents, illnesses, and unexpected circumstances can occur anywhere, making it crucial to be well-prepared.

One of the most important aspects of travel insurance is medical coverage, which ensures that travelers have access to necessary healthcare services without facing exorbitant costs. While Italy has an excellent healthcare system, medical treatment for non-residents can be expensive, especially if hospitalization or emergency procedures are required. Visitors from the European Union who hold a European Health Insurance Card (EHIC) or its updated version, the Global Health Insurance Card (GHIC) for UK travelers, can receive basic medical care in Italy at reduced or no cost. However, these cards do not cover private healthcare, repatriation, or all medical expenses, making additional insurance highly recommended. For non-EU travelers, comprehensive travel medical insurance is even more critical, as medical costs can add up quickly, particularly for services such as ambulance transportation, specialist consultations, or surgical procedures. A good policy should include coverage for doctor visits, hospital stays, prescription medications, and emergency evacuation if specialized treatment is required elsewhere.

In addition to medical coverage, trip cancellation and interruption insurance can protect travelers from financial losses if unforeseen circumstances force them to change or cancel their plans. Flights, accommodations, and tours often have strict cancellation policies, and non-refundable bookings can result in significant losses if a trip is cut short due to illness, injury, or other emergencies. Travel insurance can reimburse costs related to canceled flights, missed connections, or sudden changes due to personal or family emergencies. This type of coverage is particularly useful for those booking high-cost trips, extended stays, or travel during unpredictable weather seasons when flight disruptions are more common.

Lost, stolen, or damaged belongings can be another major inconvenience during travel, and baggage insurance can help cover the costs of replacing essential items. While Sardinia is generally a safe destination with low crime rates, theft can occur, especially in busy tourist areas, on public transportation, or in major cities like Cagliari and Alghero. Pickpocketing, though not widespread, is a risk in crowded areas, and luggage mishandling by airlines or ferry companies can result in lost or delayed baggage. A good travel insurance policy should cover the cost of replacing lost passports, personal belongings, and essential travel items while providing assistance in securing replacements for important documents.

Adventure and activity coverage is another important aspect to consider when traveling to Sardinia, particularly for those engaging in outdoor sports or water-based activities. The island is famous for its hiking trails, rock climbing spots, diving sites, and water sports, all of which come with some level of risk. Standard travel insurance may not cover high-risk activities such as scuba diving, kitesurfing, canyoning, or mountain trekking, so it is important to check the policy's terms and conditions before purchasing. If planning to participate in adventure sports, look for a policy that specifically includes coverage for injuries or accidents related to these activities, as well as any necessary medical evacuation services in case of serious emergencies.

Car rental insurance is another key consideration for travelers planning to explore Sardinia by car. While many credit card companies offer rental car insurance, coverage can vary widely, and local car rental agencies often try to sell additional insurance at high prices. A comprehensive travel insurance plan that includes rental car coverage can help avoid unnecessary extra charges while ensuring protection against accidents, theft, or damage to the vehicle. Since Sardinia's rural roads can be narrow and winding, and local driving customs may be different from what visitors are accustomed to, having proper insurance coverage can provide peace of mind while navigating the island.

When choosing a travel insurance provider, it is essential to carefully read the policy details and compare different options to ensure adequate coverage. Some policies have exclusions for pre-existing medical conditions, specific high-risk activities, or age limits, so it is important to verify that the coverage meets individual needs. Checking the claim process and customer service availability can also be beneficial, as having 24/7 support in case of an emergency can make a significant difference in stressful situations.

Another important factor to consider is whether the insurance provider includes coverage for trip delays, emergency accommodation, and alternative transport if travel disruptions occur. While Sardinia has a reliable transportation network, flight delays, ferry cancellations due to rough seas, or unexpected strikes can affect travel plans. Insurance that reimburses additional accommodation expenses or alternative transportation costs can help travelers manage unexpected delays without incurring substantial out-of-pocket expenses.

For those traveling with valuable electronics, such as cameras, smartphones, or laptops, additional coverage for expensive items may be necessary. Standard travel insurance policies often have limits on claims for personal belongings, so travelers carrying high-value equipment should check if they need supplemental coverage to protect against theft, loss, or accidental damage.

Finally, ensuring that the policy provides emergency assistance services, including access to a 24-hour helpline, translation support, and assistance with medical referrals, can be crucial in case of an emergency. Many reputable travel insurance providers offer direct billing arrangements with hospitals, eliminating the need for travelers to pay out of pocket and seek reimbursement later. Having a clear understanding of how to file claims, what documentation is required, and how quickly reimbursements are processed can prevent unnecessary stress in case of an incident.

Travel insurance is an essential part of trip planning, providing financial protection, access to medical care, and assistance in case of emergencies. While many travelers hope never to need their insurance, having the right coverage can make a significant difference if unexpected situations arise. Whether visiting Sardinia for relaxation, adventure, or cultural exploration, investing in a reliable travel insurance policy ensures peace of mind, allowing visitors to focus on enjoying their journey without worrying about potential risks.

Packing Guide

Packing for a trip to Sardinia requires careful consideration of the island's climate, activities, and cultural norms to ensure a comfortable and enjoyable experience. Since Sardinia offers a diverse range of landscapes and experiences, from sun-soaked beaches and rugged mountains to historic towns and vibrant nightlife, having the right essentials in your luggage can make all the difference. A well-thought-out packing checklist will help travelers prepare for different weather conditions, planned excursions, and any unexpected situations that may arise. Whether visiting in peak summer, mild spring and autumn, or during the quiet winter months, packing appropriately for Sardinia will enhance the travel experience and ensure that visitors are well-prepared for their adventures.

The foundation of any Sardinia packing list starts with clothing that suits the season and activities planned during the trip. Lightweight, breathable fabrics such as cotton and linen are ideal for the summer months when temperatures can soar above 30°C (86°F). T-shirts, shorts, sundresses, and loose-fitting outfits will help travelers stay cool while exploring the island. A swimsuit is an absolute must, as Sardinia is home to some of the most stunning beaches in the Mediterranean, and whether lounging on the sand, snorkeling in crystal-clear waters, or embarking on a boat tour, visitors will likely find themselves spending plenty of time near the sea. For those planning to visit high-end beach clubs or dine at upscale restaurants along the Costa Smeralda, a stylish cover-up or a light summer dress will come in handy to maintain a refined look when transitioning from beachwear to casual chic.

Comfortable footwear is another essential packing item, as exploring Sardinia often involves a mix of beach walks, city strolls, and nature hikes. Sandals or flip-flops are perfect for the beach, but travelers should also bring a pair of sturdy walking shoes or sneakers for exploring towns, archaeological sites, and rural landscapes. For those planning to hike in the Gennargentu mountains or along the island's scenic coastal trails, durable hiking shoes with good grip are highly recommended. Many of Sardinia's most picturesque beaches, such as Cala Goloritzé and Cala Luna, require a short trek to access, so appropriate footwear will ensure a more comfortable and safe experience.

Sun protection is a critical consideration when visiting Sardinia, particularly during the summer months when the Mediterranean sun is at its strongest. A high-SPF sunscreen is a must-have to protect the skin from sunburn, and a wide-brimmed hat, sunglasses with UV protection, and a light scarf or shawl for added sun coverage can help prevent overexposure. Sardinia's beaches can be quite exposed with minimal shade, making sun protection even more essential for those spending long hours outdoors. Travelers should also carry a reusable water bottle to stay hydrated, as the combination of heat and outdoor activities can quickly lead to dehydration.

For those visiting Sardinia outside of the peak summer months, layering is key to adjusting to the changing temperatures throughout the day. Spring and autumn bring pleasant but sometimes unpredictable weather, so packing a mix of short-sleeved shirts, light sweaters, and a waterproof jacket will ensure comfort in varying conditions. Evenings can be cool, especially in the mountainous regions and rural areas, so a lightweight jacket or cardigan will be useful for nighttime excursions. Winter travelers should pack warmer clothing, including sweaters, a coat, and possibly gloves and scarves if venturing into the island's higher elevations, where temperatures can drop significantly, and occasional snowfall occurs.

Beyond clothing, practical accessories and travel essentials will help enhance the Sardinian experience. A daypack or small backpack is useful for carrying essentials while exploring, whether on a day trip to a remote beach, a hike through the island's rugged terrain, or a sightseeing tour of a historic city. A waterproof dry bag is also a great investment for those planning to spend a lot of time near the water, keeping valuables like phones, wallets, and cameras safe from splashes during boat trips or kayaking adventures.

A good-quality camera or smartphone with ample storage is a must to capture Sardinia's breathtaking scenery, from the dramatic cliffs of the east coast to the golden sunsets over Alghero. Travelers who enjoy photography may also want to bring a portable tripod for stunning landscape shots, particularly in less touristy areas where the beauty of Sardinia remains untouched. Additionally, power banks and international adapters are important for keeping electronic devices charged, as Italy uses Type F and Type L power sockets, which may not be compatible with chargers from other countries.

For those planning to explore Sardinia's culture and history, a small guidebook or offline travel app can be helpful, especially when navigating remote areas where internet connectivity may be limited. Learning a few basic Italian phrases or downloading a translation app can also be useful, as English is not as widely spoken in smaller villages and rural areas compared to major cities and tourist hubs. Sardinia has a distinct cultural identity, and making an effort to communicate with locals, even with simple greetings or questions, can enhance the travel experience and create meaningful connections.

Beachgoers may also want to pack additional items such as a lightweight beach towel, snorkeling gear, and water shoes for exploring rocky coves and hidden sea caves. While many tour operators provide snorkeling equipment for excursions, bringing personal gear ensures better fit and hygiene. A small picnic set or reusable containers can be useful for enjoying local delicacies on the go, as Sardinia is known for its fresh, flavorful foods that can be enjoyed outdoors, whether at a scenic overlook or along a quiet stretch of coastline.

Those planning to rent a car and explore the island independently should remember to bring their driver's license and an International Driving Permit if required. While driving in Sardinia is relatively straightforward, having a GPS or offline maps app can be extremely helpful, as some rural roads lack clear signage, and mobile reception may be inconsistent in remote areas. Keeping a printed copy of important documents, including travel insurance details, accommodation confirmations, and emergency contacts, is also recommended in case of technical issues with digital devices.

A small first-aid kit is another practical addition to any Sardinia packing list, containing essentials such as band-aids, antiseptic wipes, pain relievers, motion sickness tablets for boat trips, and any necessary prescription medications. Pharmacies are widely available in Sardinia, but having immediate access to basic medical supplies can be convenient, especially when exploring more remote locations.

By packing thoughtfully and considering the island's climate, activities, and cultural nuances, travelers can ensure a comfortable and stress-free experience in Sardinia. Whether relaxing on the beach, hiking through dramatic landscapes, or immersing in the island's rich history, having the right essentials on hand will enhance the journey and allow visitors to fully enjoy everything this Mediterranean gem has to offer. Planning ahead and packing efficiently will help travelers focus on creating unforgettable memories rather than dealing with unnecessary inconveniences, ensuring a seamless and enjoyable adventure in Sardinia.

Health & Safety Tips

When traveling to Sardinia, it is essential to prioritize health and safety to ensure a smooth and enjoyable trip. While the island is a generally safe destination with a high standard of healthcare, being prepared for potential health concerns, knowing emergency contacts, and respecting local customs will contribute to a worry-free experience. Travelers should take certain precautions before their trip, including checking vaccination requirements, carrying necessary medications, and familiarizing themselves with local safety guidelines. Understanding how to respond to medical emergencies, knowing whom to contact in case of an issue, and being aware of Sardinia's cultural etiquette will help visitors feel more comfortable and well-prepared.

Before traveling to Sardinia, visitors should ensure that their routine vaccinations are up to date. While there are no mandatory vaccines required for entry into Italy, it is recommended that travelers be vaccinated against common diseases such as measles, mumps, and rubella (MMR), diphtheria, tetanus, and pertussis (DTP), as well as hepatitis A and B, particularly if planning to stay for an extended period or engage in activities that may increase exposure. While the risk of contracting serious illnesses in Sardinia is low, those who plan to hike in rural areas or spend time in nature should also consider getting vaccinated for tick-borne encephalitis, as ticks are present in some wooded regions. Rabies is rare in Sardinia, but those who may have close contact with animals, such as veterinarians or wildlife researchers, should discuss the need for a rabies vaccination with their doctor. Influenza shots are recommended for travelers visiting during flu season, particularly for older individuals or those with pre-existing health conditions.

Carrying a basic travel health kit can be useful for minor medical issues, particularly when exploring remote areas where pharmacies may not be easily accessible. The kit should include essential medications such as pain relievers, antihistamines for allergies, motion sickness tablets for ferry rides or boat excursions, and any personal prescription medications in their original packaging. It is also advisable to carry antiseptic wipes, band-aids, and rehydration salts, especially during the hot summer months when dehydration can be a concern. While Sardinia has modern medical facilities, bringing necessary medications from home ensures that travelers have access to familiar and reliable treatments without the need for immediate pharmacy visits.

In the event of a medical emergency, knowing the appropriate contacts can be crucial. The general emergency number in Italy, including Sardinia, is 112, which connects callers to police, fire, and ambulance services. For medical emergencies, travelers can also dial 118 for immediate assistance from paramedics and emergency responders. The number for police assistance is 113, while 115 connects to the fire department. Pharmacies are widely available across Sardinia, and many operate on a rotating schedule to provide 24-hour service in major cities. Signs with a green cross indicate pharmacies, and many display a schedule showing which nearby locations are open outside of normal business hours. In case of a non-emergency medical issue, travelers can visit a local Guardia Medica (out-of-hours medical center) for assistance, particularly in smaller towns where hospitals may not be nearby. Major cities such as Cagliari, Sassari, and Olbia have well-equipped hospitals and private clinics that provide high-quality care, and visitors from the European Union can use their European Health Insurance Card (EHIC) or Global Health Insurance Card (GHIC) to receive medical treatment at reduced costs.

Travelers should also take basic safety precautions while exploring Sardinia. Although the island has a low crime rate compared to other tourist destinations, petty theft and pickpocketing can occur in crowded areas, particularly in busy markets, public transport hubs, and popular tourist sites. It is advisable to keep valuables secure, use anti-theft bags, and avoid carrying large amounts of cash. ATMs are widely available, and credit cards are accepted in most establishments, so there is no need to carry excessive cash. Travelers should also be cautious when using public Wi-Fi in tourist areas and consider using a VPN for added security when accessing sensitive information.

Sardinia is known for its stunning natural landscapes, but visitors should be mindful of outdoor safety. During the summer months, extreme heat can pose a risk, particularly for those hiking or spending extended periods in direct sunlight. It is essential to stay hydrated, wear sunscreen, and take breaks in shaded areas to prevent heat exhaustion. Travelers engaging in outdoor activities such as hiking in the Supramonte mountains, exploring caves, or swimming in remote beaches should inform someone of their plans and carry a mobile phone with emergency contacts. While Sardinia's beaches are beautiful, some have strong currents, and not all are patrolled by lifeguards. Paying attention to posted warning signs, avoiding swimming in rough waters, and being aware of jellyfish presence in certain areas will help ensure a safe beach experience.

Respecting local customs and traditions is an important aspect of traveling to Sardinia. The island has a unique cultural identity that blends Italian and Sardinian heritage, and while locals are generally warm and welcoming, understanding basic etiquette can enhance interactions. Dress codes are relaxed at the beach but more conservative in towns and religious sites. When visiting churches, monasteries, or historical landmarks, covering shoulders and wearing appropriate attire is appreciated. Greetings are important in Sardinian culture, and a friendly "Buongiorno" (good morning) or "Buonasera" (good evening) when entering shops or restaurants is a sign of respect. Dining etiquette follows Italian traditions, with meals being a social experience. Tipping is not obligatory but is appreciated for good service, and it is common to round up the bill rather than leaving a fixed percentage.

Sardinia's pace of life is more relaxed compared to mainland Italy, particularly in rural villages where businesses may close for several hours in the afternoon for the traditional "riposo" or siesta. Travelers should plan around this schedule, as many small shops and restaurants may be closed between 1:00 PM and 4:00 PM before reopening for the evening. Patience and flexibility are key when navigating the local rhythm of life, and adapting to the island's slower pace can be part of the charm of visiting Sardinia.

For travelers driving in Sardinia, road safety should be a priority. While main highways are well-maintained, some rural roads can be narrow, winding, and poorly lit at night. Driving with caution, following speed limits, and being aware of local driving habits will help ensure a safe journey. Renting a car is the best way to explore the island, but visitors should be mindful that in smaller villages, parking can be limited, and local traffic regulations should be followed to avoid fines.

Staying informed about local laws and regulations will also contribute to a hassle-free experience. Certain beaches and protected areas have restrictions to preserve the environment, such as limits on bringing away sand or shells. Violating these rules can result in fines, so respecting conservation efforts is important. Smoking is prohibited in certain public areas, and waste disposal follows strict recycling guidelines in many towns. Understanding and adhering to these rules helps support sustainable tourism and shows respect for the island's environment and culture.

Ensuring good health and safety while visiting Sardinia involves a combination of preparation, awareness, and cultural respect. By taking necessary health precautions, knowing emergency contacts, and embracing local customs, travelers can have a rewarding and worry-free experience on the island. Sardinia's welcoming atmosphere, breathtaking landscapes, and rich heritage make it a fantastic destination for all types of visitors, and with the right approach to health and safety, exploring the island can be both enjoyable and secure.

Common Sardinian Phrases

While Italian is the official language of Sardinia, the island has a distinct linguistic identity that sets it apart from mainland Italy. Sardinian, or "Sardu," is a unique Romance language with influences from Latin, Spanish, and Catalan, spoken by many locals, particularly in rural areas and smaller towns. Although most Sardinians understand and speak standard Italian, and younger generations are increasingly familiar with English, visitors may still encounter situations where a basic understanding of key phrases can be helpful. Learning some essential Sardinian expressions, along with common Italian phrases, can enhance interactions with locals, show cultural appreciation, and make navigating the island a smoother experience.

Sardinian is not a single standardized language but consists of multiple dialects that vary depending on the region. The two main dialect groups are Campidanese, spoken in the southern part of the island, including Cagliari, and Logudorese, which is prevalent in central and northern Sardinia. In Alghero, a unique variation of Catalan, known as Algherese, is spoken due to the island's historical ties to Catalonia. While visitors do not need to master these dialects to communicate effectively, recognizing common words and greetings can go a long way in making connections with locals, especially in rural villages where Sardinian is still the primary language spoken at home.

For everyday interactions, it is most practical for visitors to focus on basic Italian phrases, as nearly all Sardinians are fluent in Italian. Greetings are an essential part of daily life, and a simple "Buongiorno" (Good morning) or "Buonasera" (Good evening) when entering a shop or restaurant is considered polite. "Ciao" is commonly used among friends and in informal settings, while "Arrivederci" is a more appropriate farewell in professional or unfamiliar situations. When meeting someone for the first time, saying "Piacere" (Nice to meet you) is a friendly way to acknowledge the introduction. If a visitor wants to use a Sardinian greeting, "Bonas dies" (Good morning) in Logudorese or "Bongiornu" in Campidanese can impress locals who appreciate efforts to engage with their linguistic heritage.

When ordering food at restaurants or cafés, knowing some key phrases can make the experience smoother. "Vorrei…" (I would like…) is a useful way to request something, such as "Vorrei un caffè" (I would like a coffee). To ask for the menu, "Il menu, per favore" (The menu, please) is commonly understood, and "Il conto, per favore" (The bill, please) is useful when requesting to pay. Since Sardinia has a rich culinary tradition, learning the names of popular dishes like "porceddu" (roast suckling pig) or "culurgiones" (stuffed pasta) can help in making meal selections. If dietary restrictions are a concern, phrases like "Sono vegetariano/a" (I am vegetarian) or "Senza glutine" (Gluten-free) can be helpful in ensuring the right food choices.

Shopping in Sardinia, especially in local markets, can be an enjoyable experience, and knowing basic transactional phrases can make interactions with vendors more pleasant. "Quanto costa?" (How much does it cost?) is a common question when inquiring about prices, while "Accettate carte di credito?" (Do you accept credit cards?) is useful for those preferring not to carry too much cash. In smaller towns and markets, cash is often preferred, so having some euros on hand is recommended. If trying on clothes in a shop, asking "Posso provarlo?" (Can I try it on?) can be helpful, and when deciding to buy something, "Lo prendo" (I'll take it) signals to the vendor that you are making a purchase.

When using public transportation, understanding basic phrases can make getting around easier. "Dove si trova la stazione?" (Where is the station?) or "A che ora parte l'autobus per Cagliari?" (What time does the bus to Cagliari leave?) can be useful when navigating the bus and train networks. If needing directions, "Mi può aiutare?" (Can you help me?) is a polite way to seek assistance. Since many road signs and official notices are in Italian, familiarizing oneself with directional words like "destra" (right), "sinistra" (left), and "dritto" (straight ahead) can be beneficial.

For travelers looking to engage with locals in more personal interactions, expressing gratitude and politeness is key. "Grazie" (Thank you) and "Prego" (You're welcome) are commonly used in all situations, while "Per favore" (Please) is a good way to make requests more courteous. In Sardinian, "Gratzias" is used for thank you in Logudorese, while "Atobiu" means goodbye. A simple "Scusi" (Excuse me) or "Mi dispiace" (I'm sorry) can be helpful when navigating busy areas or making a mistake in conversation.

For those who want to show a deeper appreciation for the Sardinian language and culture, learning a few traditional expressions can be a great way to connect with locals. The phrase "A si biri" (See you later) is commonly used among friends, and "Beni, gratzias" (I'm fine, thank you) is a friendly way to respond to inquiries about well-being. Some Sardinian proverbs reflect the island's deep-rooted traditions, such as "Su tempus est oro" (Time is gold), which emphasizes the value of patience and living at a slower pace.

While English is spoken in many tourist areas, especially in hotels, restaurants, and major attractions, it is less common in rural areas and among older generations. Having a translation app or phrasebook can be helpful when venturing off the beaten path. Sardinians generally appreciate when visitors make an effort to speak Italian or Sardinian, even if only a few words, as it shows respect for the local culture. In cases where language barriers exist, using gestures or pointing at items on a menu or map can be effective in communicating needs.

Learning key Sardinian phrases and Italian expressions enhances the travel experience by fostering deeper connections with locals and making daily interactions smoother. Whether greeting a shop owner, ordering traditional dishes, or asking for directions, even a small effort in speaking the language can be met with warmth and appreciation. Sardinia's linguistic diversity is a reflection of its rich history, and engaging with it in even a simple way can enrich a traveler's journey, making the experience more immersive and rewarding.

CHAPTER 2: GETTING TO AND AROUND SARDINIA

Arriving by Air

Flights to Sardinia provide convenient and efficient access to the island from various domestic and international locations. Sardinia is served by three main airports—Cagliari Elmas Airport (CAG) in the south, Olbia Costa Smeralda Airport (OLB) in the northeast, and Alghero-Fertilia Airport (AHO) in the northwest. These airports connect the island to mainland Italy and a range of European cities, making it relatively easy for travelers to reach Sardinia by air. The choice of airport depends on the traveler's destination on the island, as well as the available flight routes from their point of origin.

Cagliari Elmas Airport (CAG) is the largest and busiest airport in Sardinia, handling both domestic and international flights. It serves as the primary gateway to the island, particularly for those visiting southern Sardinia, including the capital city, Cagliari, and the stunning beaches of Villasimius and Chia. The airport operates year-round, with flights from major Italian cities such as Rome, Milan, Naples, and Venice, as well as international connections to cities like London, Paris, Madrid, and Berlin. Airlines such as ITA Airways, Ryanair, easyJet, Volotea, and Wizz Air offer frequent services to and from

Cagliari. During the summer months, the number of flights increases significantly to accommodate the high volume of tourists, with seasonal routes added from various European locations. Flight prices vary depending on the time of year, with off-season one-way flights from mainland Italy typically costing between €30 and €80, while peak-season prices can rise to €150 or more. International flights from European cities generally range from €50 to €250, depending on the airline, booking time, and travel season.

Olbia Costa Smeralda Airport (OLB) is the primary airport for travelers heading to the northeastern part of Sardinia, including the glamorous Costa Smeralda, La Maddalena Archipelago, and the town of San Teodoro. The airport is known for handling a large number of seasonal flights, particularly during the summer, when visitors flock to the region for its luxurious resorts and pristine beaches. Domestic flights from Rome, Milan, and Bologna are available year-round, while international flights from destinations such as London, Zurich, Amsterdam, and Frankfurt operate primarily between May and October. Airlines such as Air Dolomiti, British Airways, Lufthansa, Eurowings, and Jet2 offer direct routes to Olbia. Flight prices tend to fluctuate based on demand, with one-way domestic flights starting at around €40 in the off-season and rising to €180 or more in peak summer months. International flights typically range from €70 to €300, with premium airlines offering higher-priced options that include added amenities. Due to the airport's proximity to luxury resorts, private jet services also operate from Olbia, catering to high-end travelers seeking exclusive access to the Costa Smeralda.

Alghero-Fertilia Airport (AHO) is located in the northwest of Sardinia and serves as the main entry point for those visiting Alghero, Bosa, Stintino, and the surrounding coastal regions. While smaller than Cagliari and Olbia airports, Alghero still receives a significant number of flights, particularly during the summer tourist season. The airport provides domestic flights to major Italian cities such as Rome, Milan, and Turin, as well as international connections to cities including Barcelona, Brussels, Edinburgh, and Stockholm. Ryanair, easyJet, Volotea, and Vueling are some of the primary airlines operating flights to and from Alghero. Ticket prices for domestic flights generally start at around €25 during low season and can increase to over €120 in peak travel months. International flights range from approximately €60 to €250, with costs varying based on demand and booking time.

Travelers flying to Sardinia from outside of Europe typically need to connect through a major Italian or European hub. Rome Fiumicino Airport (FCO) and Milan Malpensa Airport (MXP) are the primary connecting points for long-haul travelers, offering multiple daily flights to all three Sardinian airports. Other European hubs such as Frankfurt, Paris Charles de Gaulle, and Madrid-Barajas also provide connections to Sardinia, making it accessible from almost anywhere in the world with one or two layovers. Major airlines such as ITA Airways, Lufthansa, Air France, and British Airways provide these connecting flights, with total travel costs varying based on distance, season, and airline choice.

Flights to Sardinia operate throughout the year, but availability and frequency depend heavily on the season. The summer months, from May to September, see the highest number of flights, with additional routes introduced by low-cost carriers to accommodate increased demand. This is also the period when flights are most expensive, particularly in July and August, when tourism reaches its peak. Booking flights in advance—preferably several months ahead—is highly recommended for those traveling during peak season to secure the best fares and preferred flight schedules. During the off-season, from November to March, flight options decrease, and some routes are temporarily suspended, making it necessary to plan accordingly if visiting Sardinia outside the summer months.

In terms of flight duration, travel times from mainland Italy to Sardinia are relatively short. Flights from Rome to any of Sardinia's airports take approximately one hour, while flights from Milan last around 90 minutes. Direct flights from other European cities typically range between two to three hours, depending on departure location. Travelers should note that while flights are short, airport transfers and check-in procedures can add additional time to the journey. Public transportation options such as buses and taxis are available at all three Sardinian airports to facilitate onward travel to hotels and other destinations. Car rental services are also widely available at each airport, providing flexibility for those planning to explore the island independently.

For travelers looking for cost-effective options, budget airlines such as Ryanair, easyJet, and Volotea often provide the lowest fares, especially when booked in advance. These airlines frequently offer promotional deals on flights to Sardinia, with fares as low as €20 for one-way tickets during sales periods. However, budget carriers typically charge extra for baggage, seat selection, and other services, so travelers should factor in additional costs when comparing prices. For those seeking a more comfortable flying experience, full-service airlines such as ITA Airways, Lufthansa, and British Airways offer higher-tier options with additional amenities, including checked baggage, in-flight meals, and priority boarding.

Choosing the best flight to Sardinia depends on the traveler's budget, preferred airport, and time of year. Booking early, considering alternative routes, and being flexible with travel dates can help secure better deals and a more convenient itinerary. Whether arriving for a relaxing beach vacation, a cultural exploration, or an adventure-filled trip, Sardinia's well-connected air travel network ensures that visitors can reach the island efficiently and begin their journey in one of Italy's most captivating destinations.

Ferries Travel

Ferries to Sardinia provide an alternative and often scenic way to reach the island, particularly for those traveling from mainland Italy or other parts of the Mediterranean. Many visitors opt for ferry travel instead of flights, especially if they are bringing a car, motorcycle, or camper van, as ferries allow travelers to explore Sardinia at their own pace without the need for a rental vehicle upon arrival. The island is well-connected to the Italian mainland through several major ports, with multiple ferry operators running regular services throughout the year. The ferry routes vary in terms of duration, price, and amenities, making it important for travelers to choose the most suitable option based on their itinerary, budget, and preferences.

Sardinia has several main ferry ports that connect to various locations on the Italian mainland. The primary ports on the island include Cagliari in the south, Olbia and Golfo Aranci in the northeast, Porto Torres in the northwest, and Arbatax on the eastern coast. These ports receive ferries from different Italian cities such as Genoa, Livorno, Civitavecchia (near Rome), Naples, and Palermo, as well as international routes from France, Spain, and Corsica. The duration of the ferry journey varies depending on the departure and arrival ports, with some crossings taking as little as five hours, while others require an overnight trip.

Several ferry companies operate routes to Sardinia, offering different levels of comfort and service. Some of the most well-known ferry operators include Tirrenia, Moby Lines, Grimaldi Lines, GNV (Grandi Navi Veloci), and Corsica Ferries. Each company provides various types of vessels, including standard ferries, high-speed ferries, and luxury cruise-style ferries, allowing travelers to choose based on their preferences. Tirrenia and Moby Lines are among the most popular operators, providing frequent connections between Sardinia and the mainland with modern ships equipped with cabins, restaurants, lounges, and entertainment areas. Grimaldi Lines and GNV focus more on long-distance routes and offer competitive pricing, while Corsica Ferries operates connections between Sardinia and Corsica, as well as France and mainland Italy.

The cost of ferry travel to Sardinia depends on several factors, including the route, type of seating or cabin, vehicle transport, and the time of year. One-way tickets for foot passengers typically start at around €30 to €50 for standard seating on shorter routes, while longer crossings or premium seating options may cost between €60 and €100. Travelers who opt for a private cabin can expect to pay anywhere from €80 to €250 per cabin, depending on the level of comfort and size. Bringing a vehicle significantly increases the cost, with prices for a standard car ranging from €50 to €150 per journey, depending on the season and ferry company. Motorcycles and bicycles are generally cheaper to transport, with rates starting at around C30. Camper vans and larger vehicles have higher fees, often exceeding €200 per trip. Discounts are often available for early bookings, round-trip tickets, and group travel, while some ferry companies offer promotional fares during off-peak seasons.

Ferry schedules vary throughout the year, with more frequent crossings during the summer months when demand is at its highest. During peak season, which runs from June to September, most ferry operators increase the number of daily departures to accommodate the large influx of tourists. Some routes operate multiple times per day, particularly on high-traffic crossings such as Civitavecchia to Olbia or Genoa to Porto Torres. Overnight ferries are a popular choice for longer journeys, allowing travelers to sleep in cabins and arrive in Sardinia the following morning. These ferries typically depart in the evening and arrive early the next day, making them a convenient option for those who want to maximize their time on the island. During the winter months, ferry schedules are reduced, with some seasonal routes temporarily suspended. Travelers visiting Sardinia during the off-season should check ferry timetables in advance to ensure availability.

Boarding procedures for ferries to Sardinia are generally straightforward, but travelers should plan to arrive at the port well in advance, particularly during peak season when queues can be long. It is recommended to check in at least 90 minutes before departure for foot passengers and at least two hours before departure for those traveling with vehicles. Many ferry companies provide online check-in options, allowing passengers to receive their boarding passes digitally and avoid waiting in line at the terminal. While most ferries offer ample space for luggage, it is advisable to carry essential items in a small bag, as accessing the vehicle deck during the journey may not be allowed once the ferry is underway.

Onboard amenities vary depending on the ferry company and vessel. Most ferries to Sardinia are well-equipped with restaurants, bars, and lounges where passengers can relax during the journey. Some larger vessels feature cinemas, play areas for children, and even swimming pools, making the crossing more enjoyable, particularly for families. Cabins range from basic bunk-bed accommodations to luxury suites with private bathrooms and sea views. For budget-conscious travelers, reclining seats in shared lounges are a more affordable alternative to cabins, although they may not offer the same level of comfort for overnight trips. Wi-Fi is available on many ferries, though it may be limited in speed and coverage, particularly in open waters. Travelers who plan to work or stay connected during the journey should consider downloading necessary content beforehand or purchasing a Wi-Fi package if offered.

For those traveling with pets, most ferry companies allow animals on board, but policies vary regarding where pets are permitted during the journey. Some ferries offer pet-friendly cabins, while others require animals to stay in designated kennel areas. Passengers should check the specific pet policies of their chosen ferry operator and ensure they have any necessary documents, such as vaccination records and pet passports if traveling from outside Italy.

Choosing the best ferry route depends on the traveler's itinerary and preferred port of entry in Sardinia. The route from Civitavecchia to Olbia is one of the most popular and frequently operated crossings, providing easy access to northern Sardinia. The journey typically takes between five and eight hours, depending on the vessel type. Genoa to Porto Torres is another common route, ideal for travelers coming from northern Italy, with overnight crossings lasting approximately 10 to 12 hours. Naples to Cagliari is the primary route for those visiting southern Sardinia, with a travel time of around 15 hours, making it an ideal overnight option. Palermo to Cagliari is a less frequent but convenient route for those traveling from Sicily. Additionally, ferry routes from France, such as Marseille to Porto Torres, and from Spain, such as Barcelona to Porto Torres, provide international connections to the island.

For travelers who want to combine a visit to Sardinia with a trip to Corsica, ferry services between the two islands operate regularly. Corsica Ferries and Moby Lines provide crossings between Bonifacio and Santa Teresa Gallura, with a short travel time of approximately one hour. This route is a great option for those looking to explore both islands without the need for additional flights.

Ferries to Sardinia offer a flexible and enjoyable way to reach the island, particularly for travelers who want to bring their own vehicles or experience a scenic sea journey. With multiple operators, a variety of routes, and a range of pricing options, travelers can choose the ferry service that best suits their needs and budget. Whether opting for a quick daytime crossing or a comfortable overnight voyage, taking a ferry to Sardinia provides a memorable start to any adventure on this stunning Mediterranean island.

Taxis

Taxis in Sardinia provide a convenient, though often expensive, mode of transportation for travelers who need to get around cities, transfer to and from airports, or reach destinations that are not easily accessible by public transport. Unlike major European cities where taxis are abundant and easy to hail on the street, in Sardinia, taxis are typically found at designated stands, booked by phone, or reserved in advance through private companies and mobile apps. The availability of taxis varies depending on location, with larger cities such as Cagliari, Olbia, Alghero, and Sassari having more taxi services, while smaller towns and rural areas may have limited or no taxi presence, requiring pre-arranged transport.

The main taxi services in Sardinia are operated by various companies, often localized to specific cities or regions. Some of the well-known taxi companies include **Radio Taxi Cagliari**, **Taxi Alghero**, **Radio Taxi Sassari**, and **Taxi Olbia**, each providing services primarily within their respective urban areas. These companies offer traditional taxi services, airport transfers, and in some cases, pre-arranged long-distance trips. Unlike in larger metropolitan areas, ride-hailing apps such as Uber and Lyft do not operate widely in Sardinia, meaning visitors must rely on official taxi services or alternative transport options. However, some local taxi operators have adopted app-based booking systems or WhatsApp for easier communication, particularly for non-Italian-speaking travelers.

Taxis are most commonly used for airport transfers, with dedicated taxi ranks at Cagliari Elmas Airport, Olbia Costa Smeralda Airport, and Alghero-Fertilia Airport. From Cagliari Elmas Airport, a taxi ride to the city center costs approximately **€20 to €25** during the day and can increase to **€30 to €35** at night due to nighttime surcharges. From Olbia Costa Smeralda Airport, a ride to Olbia city center generally costs around **€15 to €25**, while longer trips to destinations such as Porto Cervo in the Costa Smeralda region can range between **€70 and €100**, depending on the time of day and luggage requirements. Similarly, from Alghero-Fertilia Airport, a taxi ride to the city center costs approximately **€25 to €30**, with longer journeys to coastal areas such as Stintino costing upwards of **€80 to €100**.

Within city centers, taxi fares start with a base rate of around **€3 to €5**, followed by an additional charge of **€1.50 to €2 per kilometer**, depending on the company and time of travel. Night fares, which typically apply from **10:00 PM to 6:00 AM**, are subject to an additional surcharge of around **20% to 30%**, making nighttime taxi rides significantly more expensive than daytime fares. Some companies also apply extra charges for luggage, travel during public holidays, or long waits in traffic. It is important for travelers to confirm fares with the driver before starting the journey, as taxi meters should be used for most trips. However, for long-distance rides or pre-arranged transfers, fixed rates may apply, particularly for journeys to popular tourist areas or coastal resorts.

Unlike in some major European cities where taxis can be easily hailed on the street, in Sardinia, it is more common to find taxis at official stands located near airports, train stations, and central squares. In Cagliari, main taxi ranks can be found at **Piazza Matteotti** near the train station, **Via Roma**, and **Piazza Yenne**, while in Olbia, taxis are readily available at **Corso Umberto** and **Piazza Regina Margherita**. Alghero has taxi stands at **Via Catalogna** and **Piazza Sulis**, while in Sassari, taxis can be found at **Piazza Italia** and **Corso Vittorio Emanuele**. Outside of these main areas, taxis are less frequent, and travelers may need to book a ride in advance or call a local taxi service for pick-up.

For those traveling to remote locations, hiring a taxi can be costly, as many taxi companies charge additional fees for long-distance journeys outside city limits. For example, a taxi from Cagliari to Villasimius, a popular beach destination, can cost anywhere from **€80 to €120**, while a trip from Alghero to Bosa may range between **€70 and €90**. Travelers who plan to visit multiple destinations in a single day may consider arranging a private driver or taxi service with a fixed hourly rate, which can range from **€30 to €50 per hour**, depending on the company and vehicle type.

Taxis are also available for excursions and sightseeing tours, with some drivers offering personalized itineraries to explore Sardinia's scenic routes, archaeological sites, and coastal towns. While this option provides flexibility, it is generally more expensive than renting a car or taking public transport. Many taxi companies offer full-day or half-day excursions, particularly for cruise ship passengers arriving at Sardinia's main ports. Prices for these tours vary widely but typically start at around **€150 to €300**, depending on the distance covered and the number of passengers.

For travelers staying in Sardinia's smaller villages or less touristy areas, taxis may not always be readily available, and it is often necessary to arrange transportation in advance. Many rural accommodations, including agriturismi (farm stays), can assist with booking taxis or providing contact information for local drivers. In some cases, private transfer services, which operate similarly to taxis but require advance booking, can be a more reliable option for reaching remote locations.

Language barriers can sometimes be a challenge when taking taxis in Sardinia, as not all drivers speak English fluently, particularly in less touristy areas. It can be helpful for travelers to have their destination written down in Italian, along with any special requests or instructions. Using Google Translate or a translation app can also assist in communication, especially for discussing fares or routes. Some taxi companies provide English-speaking drivers upon request, though this may come at a higher cost.

Tipping taxi drivers in Sardinia is not obligatory, but rounding up the fare or leaving a small tip of **€1 to €2** for good service is appreciated. Unlike in some countries where tipping is expected, Sardinia follows the general Italian custom where service charges are often included in the fare, so passengers are not required to tip unless they wish to show extra appreciation for a particularly helpful driver.

Taxis in Sardinia provide a convenient, though sometimes costly, transportation option for visitors who need flexibility in their travel plans. While taxis are widely available in larger cities and tourist hubs, they are less common in rural areas, making advance booking essential in certain locations. The relatively high fares compared to public transport mean that taxis are best used for airport transfers, short city trips, or situations where no other transportation options are available. By understanding the pricing, booking methods, and alternative transport options, travelers can make informed decisions when using taxis in Sardinia, ensuring a smooth and stress-free travel experience.

Public Transit

Public transit in Sardinia is a mix of buses, trains, and limited urban transport services that provide connections between major cities, smaller towns, and rural areas. While the public transport system is functional, it is not as extensive or frequent as in mainland Italy, meaning that careful planning is required to navigate the island efficiently. Travelers who rely on public transit should familiarize themselves with the main transport providers, routes, schedules, and costs to ensure a smooth experience. While buses are the most widely available and practical option, trains serve key routes, and urban transport within larger cities offers some convenience for short-distance travel.

The main provider of regional bus services in Sardinia is **ARST (Azienda Regionale Sarda Trasporti)**, which operates the majority of intercity and rural bus routes. ARST buses connect all major cities, including **Cagliari, Sassari, Olbia, and Alghero**, as well as smaller towns and villages across the island. These buses are the most common form of public transport and provide access to many areas where trains do not run. Routes extend to popular tourist destinations, including **Costa Smeralda, Bosa, Stintino, Villasimius, and Santa Teresa Gallura**, making them an essential option for visitors without a car. ARST buses generally run from early morning until the evening, though services in rural areas may be infrequent, with only a few departures per day. Tickets for ARST buses are reasonably priced, with short-distance trips typically costing **€1.50 to €3**, while longer journeys, such as Cagliari to Alghero or Olbia to Sassari, range between **€8 and €15**. Tickets can be purchased at ARST bus stations, authorized newsstands, or directly from the driver, though buying in advance is recommended to secure a seat on popular routes.

Urban bus services are available in Sardinia's main cities, with Cagliari having the most extensive network, operated by **CTM (Consorzio Trasporti e Mobilità)**. CTM buses cover the **Cagliari metropolitan area, including Poetto Beach, Quartu Sant'Elena, and Elmas Airport**, providing a reliable option for getting around the city. These buses run frequently, with some key routes operating every 10-15 minutes, making them convenient for both locals and tourists. Tickets for CTM buses cost **€1.30** for a single ride or **€3.30** for a 24-hour pass, allowing unlimited travel within the urban network. Tickets can be purchased at vending machines, kiosks, and CTM ticket offices, as well as through the official CTM app, which provides real-time bus tracking and route planning.

Sassari also has an urban bus network managed by **ATP Sassari**, which operates routes within the city and its outskirts. The bus system covers key locations such as **the historic center, train station, and university area**, making it useful for students and tourists alike. Olbia has **ASPO (Azienda Servizi Pubblici Olbia)** buses that serve the city and nearby beaches, including **Pittulongu and Porto Istana**, popular among travelers looking for a budget-friendly way to reach the coast. Alghero has a smaller urban bus network operated by **ATP Alghero**, which connects **the city center, Fertilia, and Alghero Airport** with fares similar to those in other cities.

Trains in Sardinia are operated by **Trenitalia**, the national railway service, providing connections between major cities and towns. However, the railway network in Sardinia is less developed compared to mainland Italy, with limited routes and slower travel times. The main train lines run between **Cagliari and Sassari, Cagliari and Olbia, and Sassari and Porto Torres**, with stops in intermediate towns like **Oristano, Macomer, and Chilivani**. Trains in Sardinia are generally reliable but are not the fastest mode of transport, with a journey from Cagliari to Sassari taking approximately **3 to 4 hours**. Train fares are affordable, with short-distance tickets costing €2 to €5, while longer trips, such as Cagliari to Olbia, range from €15 to €25 depending on the type of train and ticket class. Trenitalia offers discounted fares for early bookings, and tickets can be purchased online, at station kiosks, or through mobile apps.

In addition to Trenitalia services, Sardinia has a **narrow-gauge railway network** operated by ARST, known as **"Trenino Verde" (Little Green Train)**, which is a scenic tourist railway rather than a standard commuter service. The Trenino Verde runs seasonal routes through **picturesque countryside, mountains, and coastal landscapes**, offering a unique way to explore Sardinia's natural beauty. The train travels through less accessible areas, including **Mandas, Laconi, Sorgono, Tempio Pausania, and Arbatax**, providing a slow but charming journey ideal for those looking for a relaxed sightseeing experience. Tickets for the Trenino Verde vary depending on the route, with prices typically ranging from **€20 to €30 per journey**. The service is highly seasonal, running primarily in summer, and schedules are limited, so advance booking is recommended.

Public transport options between Sardinia's airports and major cities vary by location. **Cagliari Elmas Airport** is well connected by train to Cagliari city center, with Trenitalia operating frequent services that take **just 6 minutes**, making it the fastest and most convenient option. The train fare is approximately **€1.30**, and departures run every **15 to 20 minutes** throughout the day. For those traveling to and from **Olbia Costa Smeralda Airport**, **ASPO bus line 10** connects the airport to the city center, with a fare of **€1.50** per ride. **Alghero-Fertilia Airport** is served by **ARST bus line 9373**, which runs to Alghero city center for around €1.50, with departures approximately every **hour**.

For intercity travel, while buses and trains are available, their schedules are often limited, and connections between smaller towns may not always be convenient. In rural areas and coastal resorts, public transport can be infrequent, particularly on weekends and holidays, when some services may not operate at all. Travelers relying on public transit should plan ahead, check schedules in advance, and consider alternative transport options such as car rentals or taxis for reaching more remote destinations.

Despite its limitations, public transit in Sardinia remains a viable option for budget-conscious travelers and those exploring major cities or well-connected tourist areas. Buses offer the widest network coverage, though they may require careful timing to align with limited schedules. Trains provide a scenic but slower way to travel between key locations, while urban transport within Sardinia's main cities offers an affordable and convenient way to navigate local areas. Travelers should always check official websites or transport apps for up-to-date schedules and availability, as services may change seasonally or be subject to unexpected delays. While public transit in Sardinia requires some patience and flexibility, with proper planning, it can be a useful way to explore the island without the need for a rental car.

Car Rental

Renting a car in Sardinia is one of the best ways to explore the island, offering visitors the freedom to travel at their own pace and reach remote areas that are difficult to access by public transport. While Sardinia does have buses and trains connecting major cities and towns, public transport schedules can be infrequent, especially in rural regions. A rental car provides flexibility, allowing travelers to explore hidden beaches, picturesque villages, and scenic mountain landscapes without being limited by public transport availability. Given the island's diverse geography, renting a car is often the most convenient option for visitors who want to experience Sardinia beyond its main tourist hubs.

Car rental services are widely available at Sardinia's main airports, including **Cagliari Elmas Airport (CAG), Olbia Costa Smeralda Airport (OLB), and Alghero-Fertilia Airport (AHO)**, as well as in major cities such as **Cagliari, Sassari, Olbia, and Alghero**. Many international and local car rental companies operate in Sardinia, providing a range of vehicle options from compact cars to SUVs and luxury vehicles. Well-known international rental companies such as **Hertz, Avis, Europcar, Sixt, Enterprise, and Budget** have offices at the airports and city centers, offering convenient pickup and drop-off locations. Additionally, local rental companies such as **Sardinia Rent a Car, Ruvioli Rent, Only Sardinia Autonoleggio, and Mistral Rent** provide competitive pricing and personalized service, sometimes with better rates than larger international brands.

The cost of renting a car in Sardinia varies depending on the type of vehicle, season, rental duration, and additional services. In the low season (October to April), prices are generally lower, with economy car rentals starting at around **€25 to €40 per day**, while mid-size cars range from **€40 to €70 per day**. During peak season (June to September), demand is significantly higher, and rental prices increase accordingly, with compact cars costing around **€50 to €80 per day**, while larger vehicles, SUVs, or automatic cars can range from **€80 to €150 per day**. Luxury cars and convertibles, which are popular in regions like Costa Smeralda, can exceed **€200 per day** in the high season. Weekly rentals often come at discounted rates, with economy cars available for around **€250 to €500 per week**, depending on the season.

Most car rental companies require drivers to be at least **21 years old**, although some companies may impose a higher minimum age of **23 or 25**, particularly for premium or high-performance vehicles. Drivers under **25** may be subject to a **young driver surcharge**, which can range from **€10 to €25 per day**, depending on the rental company. A valid driver's license is required, and non-EU travelers may need an **International Driving Permit (IDP)**, particularly if their license is not in the Latin alphabet. It is advisable to check with the rental company in advance to confirm documentation requirements.

Operating hours for car rental agencies vary, with airport rental offices generally open from **7:00 AM to 11:00 PM**, while city center locations often operate from **8:00 AM to 7:00 PM**, with a break in the afternoon for "riposo" (the

Italian siesta), particularly in smaller towns. Some rental companies offer **24-hour pickup and drop-off services**, but this may come with an additional fee. Online reservations are highly recommended, especially during the summer months when car availability is limited. Booking in advance not only ensures better rates but also provides more vehicle options, particularly for automatic cars, which are less common in Italy than manual transmissions.

When renting a car in Sardinia, travelers should carefully review the rental agreement, paying close attention to insurance coverage, fuel policies, mileage restrictions, and additional fees. Most rental cars come with **basic insurance (CDW - Collision Damage Waiver)**, which covers damages but often includes a high deductible, meaning the driver is responsible for a portion of the repair costs in case of an accident. Many rental companies offer **full coverage insurance** or **Super CDW** to reduce liability, though this can add **€10 to €30 per day** to the rental cost. Some credit cards provide rental car insurance as a benefit, so travelers should check with their card issuer before purchasing additional coverage.

Fuel policies also vary among rental companies, with some operating on a **full-to-full policy**, where travelers pick up the car with a full tank and return it full, while others use a **prepaid fuel policy**, which may be less cost-effective. Gasoline and diesel prices in Sardinia fluctuate but generally range from **€1.70 to €2.00 per liter**, meaning that refueling a car can be a significant additional expense. Fuel stations are widely available in cities and along major roads but may be harder to find in remote areas, so it is advisable to refuel before embarking on long drives.

Driving in Sardinia is relatively straightforward, but there are some important considerations to keep in mind. Roads in cities and along the coast are well-maintained, but **rural roads can be narrow, winding, and occasionally unpaved**, requiring extra caution, especially in mountainous areas. Speed limits are strictly enforced, with limits set at **50 km/h (31 mph) in urban areas, 90 km/h (56 mph) on secondary roads, and 110 km/h (68 mph) on main roads**. Sardinia does not have highways with tolls like mainland Italy, which makes driving more budget-friendly. However, many roads, particularly in the countryside, lack proper lighting at night, so extra care is needed when driving after dark.

Parking can be challenging in city centers and popular tourist destinations, especially during the high season. Many towns have **ZTL (Zona a Traffico Limitato) areas**, where only residents or authorized vehicles are allowed, and fines for unauthorized entry can be high. It is crucial to check for ZTL signs before driving into historic areas. Paid parking zones are common in cities, marked by **blue lines**, with rates ranging from **€1 to €2 per hour**, while white-lined spaces are generally free. Some coastal areas, particularly near popular beaches, have designated parking lots where daily rates can range from €5 to €15, depending on location and season.

For those planning to visit multiple regions, renting a car allows for a flexible itinerary, making it easy to explore Sardinia's diverse landscapes. Popular road trips include the **coastal drive from Cagliari to Villasimius**, the **scenic SS125 route through the Gennargentu Mountains**, and the **Alghero to Bosa coastal road**, known for its breathtaking sea views. Travelers who wish to take their rental car on a ferry to nearby islands such as **La Maddalena** should check with their rental company, as some providers prohibit ferry transport or require additional insurance.

Returning a rental car should be done with careful attention to the company's policies. Many rental agencies inspect vehicles thoroughly, and any scratches, dents, or interior damage may result in additional charges. Taking photos of the car upon pickup and drop-off can help avoid disputes. If returning the car outside of business hours, some companies provide **drop-box services** for key returns, but travelers should confirm this option in advance.

Renting a car in Sardinia is one of the best ways to experience the island's stunning scenery, charming villages, and hidden gems. While costs can be higher during peak season, early booking, careful selection of insurance options, and awareness of driving regulations can make the experience more cost-effective and enjoyable. Whether navigating the rugged coastal roads, exploring archaeological sites, or discovering remote beaches, having a rental car provides the ultimate freedom to uncover Sardinia's unique and diverse landscapes at one's own pace.

CHAPTER 3: MUST-VISIT DESTINATIONS

Costa Smeralda

Costa Smeralda, located in the northeastern region of Sardinia, is one of the most exclusive and luxurious coastal destinations in the Mediterranean. Famous for its crystal-clear turquoise waters, stunning beaches, and glamorous lifestyle, this 20-kilometer stretch of coastline is known for attracting celebrities, yacht owners, and affluent travelers from around the world. Costa Smeralda, which translates to "Emerald Coast," is part of the **Gallura region** and is best accessed from **Olbia Costa Smeralda Airport (OLB)**, which is the closest major airport. From Olbia, it takes approximately **30 to 40 minutes** by car to reach the main resort areas such as **Porto Cervo, Baia Sardinia, and Poltu Quatu**. Visitors arriving from other parts of Sardinia can drive along **the SS125** coastal road, which offers scenic views, or take the **SS131 highway** for a faster but less picturesque route. Taxis and private transfers are available from Olbia, but renting a car is highly recommended for exploring the region at one's own pace.

Costa Smeralda was developed in the **1960s by Prince Karim Aga Khan IV**, who envisioned a world-class resort destination with elegant hotels, luxury villas, and high-end amenities while preserving the area's natural beauty. Today, it remains one of the most sought-after destinations in Sardinia, blending unspoiled landscapes with exclusive resorts, upscale shopping, and a vibrant nightlife scene. The heart of Costa Smeralda is **Porto Cervo**, a prestigious marina town that serves as the center of the region's luxury tourism. Known for its **exclusive boutiques, fine dining restaurants, and private yacht clubs**, Porto Cervo is a hotspot for the international jet set, especially during the peak summer months of **July and August**, when the marina is filled with some of the world's most extravagant yachts. The town itself features elegant architecture, with pastel-colored buildings, winding streets, and a picturesque harbor that offers stunning sunset views.

One of the main attractions of Costa Smeralda is its spectacular beaches, which are often considered among the best in the Mediterranean. **Spiaggia del Principe** is one of the most famous beaches in the area, known for its soft white sand and shallow turquoise waters that make it perfect for swimming and snorkeling. This beach was said to be the favorite of Prince Aga Khan, and it remains a popular destination for visitors seeking a tranquil and scenic coastal retreat. **Capriccioli Beach**, another well-known spot, features small granite coves surrounded by lush Mediterranean vegetation, providing a serene and picturesque setting for relaxation. **Liscia Ruja**, the largest beach in Costa Smeralda, stretches for over a kilometer and is ideal for those looking for a mix of comfort and exclusivity, with several beach clubs offering sunbeds, umbrellas, and VIP services. Other notable beaches include **Romazzino Beach, Cala di Volpe, and La Celvia**, all of which offer breathtaking landscapes and excellent swimming conditions.

Beyond its beaches, Costa Smeralda is home to world-class resorts, fine dining establishments, and high-end shopping. **The Promenade du Port in Porto Cervo** is the region's premier shopping destination, featuring luxury brands such as **Gucci, Louis Vuitton, Prada, and Bulgari**, as well as art galleries and gourmet food shops. For fine dining, visitors can experience **Michelin-starred restaurants like Ristorante Cala di Volpe**, which offers exquisite Mediterranean cuisine with a focus on fresh seafood and local Sardinian ingredients. The nightlife in Costa Smeralda is equally renowned, with exclusive clubs such as **Billionaire Porto Cervo**, founded by entrepreneur Flavio Briatore, and **Phi Beach**, an open-air club that offers stunning sunset views over the sea.

For visitors interested in culture and history, Costa Smeralda offers more than just luxury and leisure. The **Stella Maris Church in Porto Cervo**, designed by architect Michele Busiri Vici, is a beautiful example of Sardinian modern architecture, featuring whitewashed walls, curved shapes, and stunning views of the marina. Nearby, the **Giants' Grave of Coddu Vecchiu**, a Bronze Age burial site, provides a glimpse into Sardinia's ancient Nuragic civilization. Another historical attraction is the **Nuraghe Albucciu**, an ancient stone structure that showcases the island's prehistoric heritage. These sites offer a fascinating contrast to the modern glamour of Costa Smeralda, allowing visitors to explore Sardinia's deep historical roots.

Outdoor enthusiasts can take advantage of Costa Smeralda's diverse activities beyond the beach. The region is known for its **excellent sailing, snorkeling, and scuba diving opportunities**, with marine reserves such as the **Maddalena Archipelago National Park** offering exceptional underwater experiences. Boat tours to **La Maddalena, Caprera, and Spargi islands** provide a chance to explore hidden coves and pristine beaches only accessible by sea. Golf lovers can visit the **Pevero Golf Club**, an 18-hole championship course that offers spectacular views of the coastline, while hikers and nature lovers can explore the **Monte Moro trail**, which leads to a panoramic viewpoint overlooking Costa Smeralda.

Costa Smeralda hosts several high-profile events throughout the year, attracting international visitors and celebrities. The **Rally Italia Sardegna**, part of the World Rally Championship, takes place in the region, offering thrilling motorsport action on Sardinia's rugged terrain. The **Porto Cervo Wine & Food Festival** is a must-visit for gastronomy enthusiasts, featuring Sardinia's finest wines, cheeses, and traditional delicacies. The **Maxi Yacht Rolex Cup**, held every September, is one of the most prestigious sailing events in the world, drawing elite sailors and luxury yacht owners to the area.

While Costa Smeralda is often associated with exclusivity and high prices, there are ways for budget-conscious travelers to enjoy the region without overspending. Visiting in the **shoulder seasons of May, June, and September** allows visitors to experience the beauty of the area without the peak summer crowds and at more affordable prices. Some public beaches remain free to access, and local trattorias in nearby towns such as **Arzachena and San**

Pantaleo offer authentic Sardinian cuisine at reasonable prices. Additionally, staying in nearby areas like **Cannigione, Golfo Aranci, or La Maddalena** can provide more budget-friendly accommodation options while still allowing easy access to Costa Smeralda's attractions.

Transportation within Costa Smeralda is primarily by car, as public transport is limited and taxis can be expensive. Renting a car is the most convenient way to explore the area, with well-maintained roads connecting the main towns and beaches. Parking can be challenging in peak season, especially in Porto Cervo, where spaces are limited and fees are high. Some resorts and luxury hotels provide shuttle services to key locations, and private boat rentals are available for those looking to explore the coastline in style.

Costa Smeralda is a destination that perfectly **combines luxury, natural beauty, cultural heritage, and outdoor adventure,** making it one of Sardinia's most iconic locations. Whether indulging in high-end shopping, dining in world-class restaurants, exploring hidden beaches, or immersing in Sardinia's ancient history, visitors to Costa Smeralda will find a unique and unforgettable experience. From its glamorous marina and five-star resorts to its untouched nature and breathtaking landscapes, Costa Smeralda remains a jewel of the Mediterranean that continues to attract travelers seeking both relaxation and adventure.

La Maddalena

La Maddalena is one of Sardinia's most breathtaking destinations, an archipelago of stunning islands known for their unspoiled beaches, crystal-clear waters, and rich history. Located in the northeastern part of Sardinia, La Maddalena consists of over **60 islands and islets**, with **La Maddalena Island** being the largest and most developed. The archipelago is a protected national park, offering visitors a chance to explore pristine landscapes, hidden coves, and some of the best snorkeling and diving spots in the Mediterranean. Its unique blend of natural beauty and historical significance makes it a must-visit for travelers seeking both adventure and relaxation.

To reach La Maddalena, visitors must take a ferry from the **port of Palau**, a coastal town in northern Sardinia. Ferries operate frequently throughout the day, with crossings taking approximately **15 to 20 minutes**. Companies such as **Delcomar and Maddalena Lines** run these services, offering regular departures every **30 to 60 minutes**. The ferry carries both passengers and vehicles, making it convenient for those renting a car to explore the archipelago at their own pace. Tickets for foot passengers cost around **€5 to €7 one way**, while vehicles cost between **€10 and €20**, depending on size. Booking in advance is generally not required except during peak summer months when demand is higher. Once on the island, visitors can navigate the town of La Maddalena and beyond by car, scooter, or bicycle, as public transport is limited.

The main town of **La Maddalena**, also called La Maddalena, is a charming seaside settlement with colorful buildings, cobbled streets, and a lively marina. The town is filled with traditional Sardinian restaurants, small boutiques, and waterfront cafés, making it a pleasant place to stroll and soak in the island's atmosphere. **Piazza Garibaldi**, the town's central square, is a great starting point, where visitors can admire historic architecture and enjoy a coffee while watching the world go by. The **Chiesa di Santa Maria Maddalena**, the island's main church, is an elegant religious site with beautiful interiors and historical artifacts linked to Admiral Horatio Nelson, who once sought refuge in La Maddalena during the Napoleonic Wars.

One of the biggest attractions of La Maddalena is its connection to **Giuseppe Garibaldi**, one of Italy's most famous historical figures. Located on the nearby island of **Caprera**, the **Garibaldi Compendium (Casa di Garibaldi)** is a must-visit site. This former home of Garibaldi, now a museum, provides insight into his life and legacy, displaying personal belongings, letters, and memorabilia. The surrounding area is also perfect for nature lovers, as Caprera is almost entirely uninhabited and covered in Mediterranean vegetation, offering fantastic hiking opportunities and panoramic viewpoints.

The **beaches of La Maddalena** are among the most spectacular in Sardinia, attracting travelers who want to experience the beauty of untouched nature. **Spiaggia Rosa (Pink Beach)** on **Budelli Island** is one of the most famous, known for its distinctive pink-hued sand caused by crushed coral and marine microorganisms. To protect its fragile ecosystem, visitors are no longer allowed to walk on the beach, but boat tours provide breathtaking views from the sea. Another remarkable beach is **Cala Coticcio**, often called "Tahiti" due to its clear turquoise waters and white sandy seabed. Located on Caprera, this beach requires a scenic hike to reach but rewards visitors with one of the most picturesque coastal spots in the entire Mediterranean.

Bassa Trinità Beach, located on La Maddalena Island, is one of the easiest to access and is ideal for families due to its shallow, calm waters. **Cala Spalmatore**, another popular beach, offers golden sands and a tranquil bay perfect for swimming and snorkeling. **Spiaggia del Relitto** (Wreck Beach) on Caprera is famous for the remains of an old shipwreck embedded in the sand, adding a unique historical element to its beauty. Many of these beaches are best explored by boat, and renting a small motorboat or joining a guided boat tour is one of the best ways to discover the archipelago's hidden gems.

For outdoor enthusiasts, La Maddalena provides excellent opportunities for **hiking, snorkeling, and diving**. The rugged landscapes of Caprera are home to trails that lead to spectacular viewpoints such as **Punta Teialone**, the highest peak in the archipelago, which offers stunning vistas over the surrounding islands and the Sardinian mainland. Snorkeling and diving are particularly rewarding in the marine park, where underwater explorers can discover vibrant coral reefs, sea caves, and a diverse array of marine life, including dolphins, groupers, and barracudas. Several local diving schools and tour operators offer excursions for both beginners and experienced divers.

The **La Maddalena Archipelago National Park**, established in **1994**, protects the rich biodiversity of the region, ensuring that its landscapes remain preserved for future generations. Covering over **12,000 hectares**, the park includes both land and sea areas, with strict regulations to minimize human impact. Visitors are encouraged to respect the environment by avoiding littering, not disturbing wildlife, and adhering to local conservation guidelines.

The best time to visit La Maddalena is between **May and October**, when the weather is warm, and the sea is ideal for swimming. July and August are the busiest months, with higher tourist numbers and more expensive accommodations, while **June and September** offer a perfect balance of good weather and fewer crowds. During the off-season, from **November to April**, ferry services continue to operate, but some tourist facilities may be closed, and the weather can be cooler and windier.

Accommodations in La Maddalena range from **luxury hotels to charming guesthouses and vacation rentals**, with options to suit different budgets. Upscale hotels such as **Grand Hotel Resort Ma&Ma** provide a high-end experience with spa services and private beach access, while **smaller boutique hotels and B&Bs** offer a more intimate atmosphere. For travelers seeking a more independent stay, vacation apartments and holiday homes can be rented in the town center or along the coast.

Dining in La Maddalena is a delightful experience, with many restaurants specializing in **fresh seafood and Sardinian cuisine**. Traditional dishes such as **spaghetti ai ricci di mare (sea urchin pasta), zuppa gallurese (a layered bread and cheese dish), and grilled fish** are must-tries. Waterfront restaurants in the town's harbor area offer stunning sunset views, creating a perfect setting for an unforgettable meal.

Getting around La Maddalena is relatively easy, with options for **car, scooter, and bicycle rentals** available near the ferry port. While the main roads are well-maintained, some coastal paths leading to secluded beaches may be unpaved, requiring extra caution when driving. For those exploring Caprera, a rental bicycle or a scenic hike is the best way to enjoy the island's natural beauty without impacting the environment.

La Maddalena is a place where history, nature, and relaxation blend seamlessly, offering visitors an unforgettable experience in one of Sardinia's most pristine locations. Whether exploring its crystal-clear beaches, hiking through rugged landscapes, discovering historical sites, or enjoying fresh seafood by the sea, La Maddalena captures the essence of the Mediterranean at its finest. Its protected national park status ensures that the beauty of the archipelago remains unspoiled, making it a paradise for those who appreciate both adventure and tranquility. With its easy accessibility, welcoming atmosphere, and endless opportunities for exploration, La Maddalena is a true gem that continues to captivate travelers seeking an authentic and breathtaking escape in Sardinia.

Ogliastra

Ogliastra is one of the most spectacular and unspoiled regions of Sardinia, located on the eastern coast of the island. Renowned for its dramatic cliffs, hidden coves, pristine beaches, and rugged mountainous landscapes, this province offers a perfect blend of coastal beauty and wild interior scenery. It is one of the least populated areas in Sardinia, making it an ideal destination for nature lovers, adventure seekers, and those looking to escape mass tourism. The region is often referred to as the "island within the island" due to its unique geography, where towering limestone mountains and dense forests meet some of the most breathtaking coastlines in the Mediterranean.

Getting to Ogliastra requires some planning, as the region does not have a major airport. The closest airport is Cagliari Elmas Airport, approximately 140 kilometers away, followed by Olbia Costa Smeralda Airport, about 170 kilometers away. From these airports, travelers can reach Ogliastra by rental car or public transport, though having a car is highly recommended due to the rural nature of the region. The main roads leading into Ogliastra are the **SS125 Orientale Sarda**, one of the most scenic drives in Sardinia, winding through the Supramonte mountains with breathtaking panoramic views, and the **SS389**, which connects Ogliastra to Nuoro and the central part of the island. While the roads are well-maintained, they can be narrow and winding, so drivers should proceed with caution, particularly at night or during inclement weather.

One of the biggest draws of Ogliastra is its incredible coastline, featuring some of the most secluded and picturesque beaches in Sardinia. **Cala Goloritzé**, a UNESCO-protected beach, is one of the most famous, known for its crystal-clear turquoise waters, white pebbled shore, and the stunning 143-meter-high limestone pinnacle that rises from the sea. Access to the beach is via a scenic hiking trail from the Golgo Plateau, which takes about an hour and offers spectacular views along the way. **Cala Mariolu**, another breathtaking beach, is accessible only by boat or a challenging hike and is famed for its mix of white sand and smooth pebbles, along with its vibrant marine life, making it a top spot for snorkeling and diving. **Cala Luna**, a crescent-shaped beach surrounded by towering cliffs and featuring large sea caves, is another must-visit, accessible by boat or through a hiking trail from Cala Fuili.

For those interested in history and archaeology, Ogliastra is home to some fascinating Nuragic sites that provide insight into Sardinia's ancient civilization. **The Nuraghe Serbissi**, perched on a hilltop overlooking the region, offers a spectacular view of the surrounding valleys and mountains. This well-preserved site consists of several stone towers and a complex system of rooms and passageways that date back over 3,000 years. Nearby, the **Domus de Janas of Monte Arista**, ancient rock-cut tombs, reveal more about the island's prehistoric past. The **Tomba dei Giganti di Osono**, a large megalithic grave attributed to the Nuragic civilization, is another important archaeological site that adds to the mystique of Ogliastra's ancient history.

Beyond its coastal beauty and archaeological wonders, Ogliastra is a paradise for outdoor enthusiasts. The **Gennargentu National Park**, which extends into Ogliastra, is home to Sardinia's highest peaks, offering incredible hiking opportunities. Trails lead through **deep gorges, dense oak forests, and high-altitude plateaus**, providing opportunities to see **wild boars, mouflons, golden eagles, and griffon vultures** in their natural habitat. One of the most famous hikes in the region is the **Gola di Gorropu**, one of the deepest canyons in Europe. The trek through Gorropu Gorge takes visitors through towering rock walls, narrow passages, and stunning geological formations, making it a challenging yet rewarding adventure. Another spectacular natural site is the **Su Marmuri Cave in Ulassai**, a vast limestone cavern featuring enormous stalactites and stalagmites, underground lakes, and awe-inspiring rock formations.

The towns and villages of Ogliastra offer a glimpse into traditional Sardinian life, with their charming streets, historic churches, and strong cultural heritage. **Tortolì**, the largest town in the region, serves as a gateway to Ogliastra's beaches and is known for its colorful murals, lively markets, and delicious seafood restaurants. The nearby coastal village of **Arbatax** is famous for its **Red Rocks (Rocce Rosse di Arbatax)**, striking red granite formations that contrast beautifully with the blue sea, making them a favorite spot for photography. Arbatax is also home to a ferry port that connects Ogliastra to mainland Italy, with services running to **Civitavecchia and Genoa**. Inland, the village of **Baunei** is perched on a mountainside and offers spectacular views of the coastline below. Baunei is also the starting point for many of the region's best hiking trails, including those leading to Cala Goloritzé and the Golgo Plateau.

Ogliastra is also known for its authentic Sardinian cuisine, with a focus on **fresh, locally sourced ingredients** and traditional recipes. One of the most famous dishes of the region is **culurgiones**, handmade pasta stuffed with **potatoes, pecorino cheese, and mint**, often served with a simple tomato sauce. The region is also known for **porceddu**, a slow-roasted suckling pig cooked over an open fire, and **su pistoccu**, a traditional flatbread similar to carasau but thicker and more rustic. Ogliastra produces some of Sardinia's finest wines, including **Cannonau**, a bold red wine that has been linked to the island's famous longevity. Local agriturismi (farm stays) provide visitors with the opportunity to taste these traditional dishes while experiencing Sardinian hospitality in a rural setting.

For those looking for unique cultural experiences, Ogliastra hosts several traditional festivals throughout the year, celebrating local history, music, and cuisine. The **Sagra delle Ciliegie (Cherry Festival) in Lanusei** is a popular event held in early summer, featuring local produce, folk music, and traditional dances. The **Sagra del Redentore in Nuoro**, which attracts visitors from across Sardinia, showcases traditional Sardinian costumes, horseback processions, and religious celebrations. Many of the smaller villages in Ogliastra also host their own local feasts, offering visitors an authentic taste of Sardinian culture.

Accommodations in Ogliastra range from **charming boutique hotels and seaside resorts to agriturismi and mountain lodges**. In coastal areas like Tortolì and Arbatax, visitors can find beachfront hotels and resorts with stunning views of the sea, while those venturing inland will discover **family-run guesthouses and rustic farm stays** that provide an immersive experience in Sardinian countryside life. Camping is also popular in Ogliastra, with campsites located near the beaches and within the forests of Gennargentu National Park.

The best time to visit Ogliastra depends on the type of activities travelers are interested in. **Summer (June to September)** is ideal for beach lovers, with warm temperatures, calm seas, and plenty of sunshine. However, this is also the busiest time of year, particularly in coastal areas. **Spring (April to June) and autumn (September to October)** offer mild weather, fewer crowds, and excellent conditions for hiking, cycling, and sightseeing. **Winter (November to March)** is the quietest season, with cooler temperatures and occasional rain, but it is still a great time for those looking to explore the cultural and historical aspects of the region without the tourist crowds.

Ogliastra is one of Sardinia's best-kept secrets, offering breathtaking natural beauty, fascinating history, and outdoor adventures in a setting that remains largely untouched by mass tourism. Whether exploring its hidden beaches, hiking through dramatic landscapes, discovering ancient archaeological sites, or experiencing authentic Sardinian traditions, visitors to Ogliastra will find a destination that feels wild, timeless, and deeply connected to the island's heritage. Its unique combination of coastal and mountain landscapes, welcoming villages, and rich culinary traditions makes it a truly unforgettable place for those seeking an authentic and adventurous Sardinian experience.

Cagliari: The Island's Capital

Cagliari, the capital of Sardinia, is a vibrant coastal city rich in history, culture, and stunning natural landscapes. Located in the southern part of the island, Cagliari serves as Sardinia's political, economic, and cultural hub, offering visitors a perfect blend of **ancient heritage, Mediterranean charm, and modern city life**. With its scenic waterfront, historic districts, lively piazzas, and beautiful beaches, the city is a must-visit destination for travelers looking to experience both urban life and seaside relaxation. Cagliari's **strategic location along the Gulf of Angels** has made it an important settlement for thousands of years, with a history shaped by Phoenicians, Romans, Pisans, Spanish rulers, and more, leaving behind a fascinating mix of architectural styles and cultural influences.

Getting to Cagliari is easy, as it is home to **Cagliari Elmas Airport (CAG)**, the largest airport in Sardinia, located just **7 kilometers** from the city center. The airport is well connected to major Italian cities such as **Rome, Milan, Venice, and Naples**, as well as international destinations like **London, Barcelona, Paris, and Munich**. From the airport, travelers can take a **direct train to Cagliari's**

central station, a journey that takes just **6 minutes** and costs around **€1.30**. Taxis and rental cars are also available for those who prefer private transportation. For visitors arriving by ferry, **Cagliari's port** welcomes ships from **Civitavecchia, Naples, and Palermo**, as well as cruise liners that stop in the city as part of Mediterranean itineraries. The **SS131 highway**, Sardinia's main road, connects Cagliari with other parts of the island, making it easily accessible by car.

The heart of Cagliari is its **historic district, Castello**, a medieval hilltop neighborhood that offers stunning panoramic views of the city and the sea. Castello is home to some of Cagliari's most iconic landmarks, including the **Bastione di Saint Remy**, a grand neoclassical structure with a large terrace providing breathtaking vistas, especially at sunset. Walking through Castello's narrow, cobbled streets reveals a mix of ancient buildings, artisan shops, and historic palaces. One of the most significant sites within Castello is the **Cagliari Cathedral (Cattedrale di Santa Maria)**, a striking 13th-century church featuring a blend of **Pisan-Romanesque, Baroque, and Gothic architectural styles**. Inside, visitors can admire elaborate frescoes, the crypt of the martyrs, and intricate sculptures.

Just outside Castello, the **Torre dell'Elefante and Torre di San Pancrazio**, two imposing medieval towers, serve as reminders of Cagliari's defensive past. These towers, built in the 14th century by the Pisans, provide incredible viewpoints over the city and are worth the climb for those looking to experience Cagliari from above. The **Roman Amphitheater**, another key attraction, dates back to the

2nd century AD and was once used for gladiator battles and public spectacles. Although partially carved into the rock, this ancient structure remains well-preserved and hosts cultural events and concerts in the summer.

For museum enthusiasts, Cagliari offers several excellent options, with the **National Archaeological Museum of Cagliari** being the most notable. This museum houses an extensive collection of **Nuragic artifacts, Phoenician relics, and Roman-era statues**, providing visitors with deep insight into Sardinia's ancient civilizations. Nearby, the **Cittadella dei Musei**, a cultural complex, includes several smaller museums and art galleries, making it an ideal stop for those interested in Sardinia's rich history.

Cagliari is also known for its stunning beaches, with **Poetto Beach** being the most famous and easily accessible. Stretching over **8 kilometers**, Poetto offers soft golden sand, crystal-clear waters, and a lively promenade lined with beach bars, seafood restaurants, and clubs. It is a popular spot for both locals and tourists, especially during the summer months, when visitors can enjoy **swimming, windsurfing, beach volleyball, and sunset aperitivos** by the sea. For a quieter beach experience, **Cala Mosca** and **Cala Fighera**, located near **Sella del Diavolo (Devil's Saddle)**, offer beautiful secluded coves surrounded by rugged cliffs, perfect for hiking and snorkeling.

Nature lovers will find plenty to explore in and around Cagliari, with **Molentargius-Saline Regional Park** being one of the city's natural highlights. This protected wetland, located between Poetto Beach and the city center, is home to a large population of **pink flamingos**, which can be observed year-round. The park offers walking and cycling trails, allowing visitors to enjoy the tranquil surroundings while spotting various bird species. Another beautiful natural site is the **Monte Urpinu Park**, a hilltop green space offering **panoramic views of the city and coastline**, as well as shaded walking paths, picnic areas, and resident peacocks.

Cagliari's food scene is a celebration of **Sardinian cuisine and fresh seafood**, with countless restaurants, trattorias, and markets offering delicious traditional dishes. Some of the must-try specialties include **fregola con arselle**, a Sardinian pasta dish with clams and a saffron-infused broth, **bottarga**, dried mullet roe often served with pasta or bread, and **malloreddus alla campidanese**, a type of gnocchi with a rich tomato and sausage sauce. The city's central market, **Mercato di San Benedetto**, is one of the largest indoor markets in Italy and a paradise for food lovers, featuring stalls selling fresh seafood, local cheeses, cured meats, and seasonal produce.

The nightlife in Cagliari is lively and diverse, offering something for every type of visitor. The **Marina district**, located near the port, is a great place to start the evening, with its **seafood restaurants, wine bars, and casual cafés**. For those looking for a more upscale experience, **Piazza Yenne** and the Castello district offer trendy cocktail bars and rooftop lounges with scenic views. During the summer, **Poetto Beach transforms into a nightlife hotspot**, with beachfront clubs and open-air music venues hosting parties that last until dawn.

Cagliari also hosts numerous festivals and cultural events throughout the year, showcasing the city's deep-rooted traditions. One of the most significant celebrations is the **Festival of Sant'Efisio**, held every **May 1st**, where thousands of people dressed in traditional Sardinian attire participate in a grand religious procession honoring Sardinia's patron saint. This festival is one of the most colorful and historic events in Sardinia, drawing visitors from across the island. Other notable events include the **Cagliari International Jazz Festival**, which brings world-class musicians to the city, and the **Regata della Madonna del Naufrago**, a unique maritime procession held in honor of sailors and fishermen.

Accommodations in Cagliari range from **luxury hotels to boutique guesthouses and budget-friendly B&Bs**, catering to all types of travelers. High-end options such as **Palazzo Doglio** offer five-star comfort, while charming boutique hotels like **Casa Clat** provide an intimate and stylish stay. Budget-conscious travelers can find well-rated guesthouses in the **Villanova and Stampace districts**, offering excellent value within walking distance of the city's main attractions.

The best time to visit Cagliari depends on personal preferences, but **spring (April to June) and autumn (September to October)** are ideal, with pleasant temperatures, fewer crowds, and comfortable conditions for sightseeing. **Summer (July to August)** is the busiest period, especially along the beaches, but it offers a vibrant atmosphere with outdoor events and festivals. **Winter (November to March)** is quieter, with mild temperatures, making it a good time for exploring the city without the tourist crowds.

Cagliari is a city that blends ancient history with modern elegance, offering visitors a rich tapestry of cultural heritage, breathtaking landscapes, beautiful beaches, lively markets, and outstanding cuisine. Whether strolling through its historic districts, sunbathing along its coastline, hiking to panoramic viewpoints, or indulging in authentic Sardinian flavors, Cagliari captures the essence of Sardinia's unique charm and warm Mediterranean spirit. Its welcoming atmosphere, scenic beauty, and cultural depth make it a destination that leaves a lasting impression on those who visit.

Alghero

Alghero, located on the **northwestern coast of Sardinia**, is one of the island's most captivating and historically rich cities. Known for its Catalan heritage, medieval old town, stunning coastline, and vibrant atmosphere, Alghero offers a perfect blend of **history, culture, and natural beauty**. Often referred to as **"Barceloneta"** due to its strong Catalan influence, Alghero is unique among Sardinian cities, as it still preserves traces of its Spanish past in its language, architecture, and traditions. The city is surrounded by **imposing defensive walls, picturesque cobbled streets, and a scenic promenade**, making it a favorite destination for visitors looking to experience a mix of history and seaside charm.

Getting to Alghero is convenient, as the city is served by **Alghero-Fertilia Airport (AHO)**, which is located just **10 kilometers** from the city center. The airport offers both **domestic and international connections**, with flights from **Rome, Milan, Bologna, and Naples**, as well as seasonal routes from **London, Paris, Barcelona, and Berlin**. From the airport, travelers can reach Alghero by **bus, taxi, or rental car**, with buses running frequently between the airport and the city center in **about 20 minutes**. For those arriving by ferry, the nearest port is **Porto Torres**, located **35 kilometers away**, with ferry connections to **Genoa, Civitavecchia, and Barcelona**. Renting a car is highly recommended for visitors who wish to explore **the surrounding coastlines, hidden beaches, and rural landscapes**, as public transport options outside the city are limited.

The **historic center of Alghero** is one of its main attractions, with **narrow, winding streets, ochre-colored buildings, and lively piazzas** filled with restaurants, cafés, and boutique shops. The **ancient city walls**, built during the Spanish rule, still stand as a testament to Alghero's strategic importance throughout history. Walking along the **Bastioni Marco Polo and Bastioni Cristoforo Colombo**, visitors can enjoy **spectacular views of the Mediterranean Sea**, especially at sunset when the sky is painted with hues of orange and pink. The **Torre del Sulis**, one of the city's well-preserved watchtowers, is an iconic symbol of Alghero and offers insight into its medieval past.

One of Alghero's most significant landmarks is the **Cattedrale di Santa Maria**, a stunning Gothic-Catalan cathedral dating back to the **16th century**. Located in the heart of the old town, the cathedral features **an impressive bell tower, intricate chapels, and a blend of Gothic, Renaissance, and Baroque architectural elements**. Another must-visit site is the **Chiesa di San Francesco**, a beautiful church with a peaceful cloister and exquisite detailing that reflects **Alghero's Spanish heritage**. The **Palazzo d'Albis**, a historic noble residence once visited by Emperor Charles V, is another notable attraction that showcases the city's **rich architectural history**.

Beyond its historic streets, Alghero is famous for its **breathtaking coastline and pristine beaches**, which are among the most beautiful in Sardinia. **Spiaggia di Maria Pia**, a long stretch of **soft white sand and shallow turquoise waters**, is located just a few kilometers from the city center and is ideal for families and sun-seekers. **Lido di San Giovanni**, Alghero's main urban beach, is easily accessible and offers beach clubs, sunbeds, and restaurants. For those looking for more secluded spots, **Mugoni Beach**, located within **Porto Conte Regional Park**, is a spectacular crescent-shaped bay with **crystal-clear water and a backdrop of pine trees**, providing a serene escape from the crowds.

A trip to Alghero would not be complete without visiting the **Neptune's Grotto (Grotta di Nettuno)**, one of Sardinia's most famous **sea caves**. Located at the base of the **Capo Caccia cliffs**, this spectacular cave is filled with **stalactites, stalagmites, and underground lakes**, creating a magical subterranean landscape. Visitors can reach Neptune's Grotto by **boat tour from Alghero's port** or by descending the **Escala del Cabirol**, a dramatic **654-step staircase** carved into the cliffs, offering breathtaking views along the way.

For nature lovers, the **Capo Caccia-Isola Piana Marine Reserve** is a paradise for **snorkeling, diving, and hiking**. The marine reserve is home to **diverse marine life, underwater caves, and dramatic cliffs**, making it a favorite spot for divers and adventure seekers. Nearby, **Porto Conte Regional Park** offers **hiking and cycling trails** through scenic landscapes of **forests, coastal cliffs, and Mediterranean vegetation**, providing opportunities to encounter **wildlife such as wild boars, falcons, and Sardinian deer**.

Alghero is also known for its unique **red coral**, which has been harvested from the local waters for centuries. The **Coral Museum (Museo del Corallo)** showcases the history and craftsmanship of Alghero's coral jewelry industry, and visitors can find **exquisite handmade coral pieces** in the town's many artisan boutiques. The city has earned the nickname **"The Coral Riviera"** due to its long-standing connection to this precious marine resource.

The **food scene in Alghero** is a delightful fusion of **Sardinian and Catalan influences**, offering a range of delicious seafood and traditional Sardinian dishes. **Lobster alla Catalana**, one of Alghero's signature dishes, consists of **fresh lobster served with tomatoes, onions, and a light dressing**, reflecting the city's Spanish roots. Other must-try dishes include **fregola ai frutti di mare**, a Sardinian pasta served with mixed seafood, **bottarga (mullet roe)** grated over pasta or served with bread, and

porceddu, the famous Sardinian **roast suckling pig**. The city's **seafront promenade and historic piazzas** are lined with excellent seafood restaurants, offering stunning sunset views alongside authentic Mediterranean flavors.

Alghero's **wine culture** is another highlight, with the region producing some of Sardinia's **finest wines**. The surrounding countryside is home to **renowned vineyards**, with **Sella & Mosca Winery** being the most famous. This historic estate offers **wine tastings and tours**, allowing visitors to sample **Cannonau, Vermentino, and Torbato**, the latter being a rare white grape variety grown primarily in the Alghero area.

Throughout the year, Alghero hosts a variety of **festivals and events**, celebrating its culture, history, and culinary traditions. The **Cap d'Any de l'Alguer (Alghero's New Year's Eve Festival)** is one of the most famous celebrations, featuring **live music, fireworks, and street performances** along the waterfront. The **Setmana Santa (Holy Week)** is a deeply traditional event influenced by Spanish customs, with **processions, religious ceremonies, and candlelit parades** through the old town. In **August, the Festival of San Michele**, the city's patron saint, brings **concerts, folk performances, and festive gatherings** to Alghero's streets.

Accommodations in Alghero range from **luxury hotels and seaside resorts to charming guesthouses and boutique B&Bs**, catering to a wide range of travelers. High-end options like **Villa Las Tronas**, a former royal retreat overlooking the sea, offer **luxurious stays with stunning views**, while **budget-friendly hotels and holiday**

apartments provide excellent options for travelers looking to explore Alghero on a more modest budget.

The best time to visit Alghero is between **May and October**, when the weather is warm, and the city is alive with events, outdoor activities, and bustling seaside life. **July and August** are the busiest months, with **higher prices and crowded beaches**, while **June and September** offer the same beauty with fewer tourists. Spring and early autumn are perfect for exploring Alghero's historic sites, hiking in nature reserves, and enjoying the beaches without the peak season crowds.

Alghero is a city that seamlessly blends history, natural beauty, Catalan heritage, and Mediterranean charm, making it one of Sardinia's most captivating destinations. Whether strolling through the medieval old town, relaxing on pristine beaches, exploring dramatic sea caves, or indulging in world-class seafood and wine, visitors will find Alghero to be an unforgettable experience that captures the essence of Sardinia's rich culture and stunning landscapes.

Oristano

Oristano, located on the **central-western coast of Sardinia**, is a historic and culturally rich city that offers visitors a unique blend of **medieval charm, archaeological treasures, beautiful beaches, and traditional festivals**. While it is often less frequented by tourists compared to Cagliari or Alghero, Oristano provides an authentic experience of **Sardinian history, cuisine, and nature**. The city is known for its well-preserved historical center, impressive churches, and proximity to some of the island's most stunning and unspoiled coastal landscapes. It is a fantastic destination for those who appreciate **history, nature, and a slower pace of life**, away from the bustling tourist crowds of Sardinia's more famous cities.

Reaching Oristano is relatively straightforward, as it is well connected by road and rail. The city lies along the **SS131 highway**, Sardinia's main arterial road that links **Cagliari in the south to Sassari in the north**. From Cagliari, Oristano is about **90 kilometers away**, making it an easy **one-hour drive**. Travelers coming from **Alghero or Sassari** can also reach Oristano via the **SS131**, with a journey time of approximately **1.5 to 2 hours**. The city is **served by a train station**, making it accessible for those traveling from **Cagliari, Olbia, and Sassari**, with regular Trenitalia services running daily. While Oristano does not have its own airport, the nearest airport is **Cagliari Elmas Airport (CAG)**, which offers both **domestic and international flights**. From the airport, visitors can either **rent a car or take a direct train** to Oristano in about an hour.

The **historic center of Oristano** is one of its main attractions, filled with **elegant piazzas, medieval architecture, and important landmarks** that reflect the city's long and fascinating history. One of the most prominent sites is the **Piazza Eleonora d'Arborea**, dedicated to **Eleonora d'Arborea**, one of Sardinia's most legendary historical figures. She was a powerful judge who ruled the **Giudicato of Arborea** in the 14th century and is best known for creating the **Carta de Logu**, an advanced legal code that remained in use in Sardinia for centuries. A **statue of Eleonora stands in the square**, surrounded by elegant buildings, shops, and cafés that make it a perfect place to relax and soak in the atmosphere.

The **Cattedrale di Santa Maria Assunta**, also known as **Oristano Cathedral**, is another significant landmark in the city. Originally built in the **13th century** and later expanded during the **Spanish period**, the cathedral boasts a **blend of Romanesque, Gothic, and Baroque elements**. Its **large dome, beautiful bell tower, and ornate interior** make it one of the most impressive churches in Sardinia. Nearby, the **Church of San Francesco** houses an important religious artifact—the **Crucifix of Nicodemus**, a stunning wooden sculpture that dates back to the **14th century** and is considered a masterpiece of medieval Sardinian art.

For those interested in Oristano's **medieval history and fortifications**, the **Torre di Mariano II**, also called the **Porta Manna**, is one of the city's most well-preserved medieval structures. Built in the **13th century**, this impressive tower was once part of Oristano's defensive walls and now serves as an iconic landmark in the city. Walking through the **narrow streets and alleys of the old town**, visitors can admire **traditional Sardinian architecture, artisan workshops, and local markets selling fresh produce, cheeses, and handcrafted goods.**

One of Oristano's most famous and unique events is the **Sartiglia**, a medieval equestrian tournament held every year on the last Sunday and Tuesday of **Carnival (February or early March)**. This historic festival, which dates back to the **16th century**, is one of the most **spectacular and ancient equestrian tournaments in Europe**. Skilled horsemen, known as **Componidori**, dressed in elaborate traditional costumes, gallop through the city's streets attempting to **spear a hanging star with their swords**, a feat that symbolizes **good fortune for the coming year**. The Sartiglia is accompanied by **music, parades, and vibrant celebrations**, making it one of the best times to visit Oristano for those looking to experience authentic Sardinian traditions.

Beyond its historical and cultural attractions, Oristano is also an excellent base for exploring some of Sardinia's most **beautiful and less crowded beaches**. Just a short drive from the city, visitors can find the **Sinis Peninsula**, a stunning natural area known for its **pristine coastline, marine biodiversity, and archaeological sites**. One of the most famous beaches in the area is **Is Arutas**, often called the **"beach of grains of rice"** because of its unique quartz sand, which sparkles under the sun. The turquoise waters and peaceful setting make it a paradise for swimming and snorkeling. Other beautiful beaches in the Sinis area include **Mari Ermi, Maimoni, and San Giovanni di Sinis**, each offering a **wild and unspoiled atmosphere** perfect for nature lovers.

The **Sinis Peninsula** is also home to **Tharros**, one of Sardinia's most important **Phoenician and Roman archaeological sites**. Founded in the **8th century BC** by the Phoenicians and later expanded by the Romans, Tharros features **ancient ruins, including columns, baths, temples, and a well-preserved road network**. Overlooking the sea, this fascinating site provides a glimpse into Sardinia's ancient past while offering spectacular views of the coastline. Close to Tharros, the **San Giovanni di Sinis Church**, one of the **oldest Christian churches in Sardinia**, dates back to the **6th century AD** and is a remarkable example of early Byzantine architecture.

For those who love **wildlife and nature**, the **Stagno di Cabras**, a large lagoon near Oristano, is a significant wetland area that serves as a habitat for numerous bird species, including **pink flamingos, herons, and cormorants**. Birdwatchers and nature enthusiasts will find this area perfect for **photography, walking trails, and observing Sardinia's rich biodiversity**. The nearby **village of Cabras** is also famous for producing **bottarga**, a delicacy made from **cured mullet roe**, which is often referred to as **"Sardinian caviar"** and is widely used in local cuisine.

Oristano is also well known for its **culinary traditions**, with a strong emphasis on **fresh seafood, locally sourced ingredients, and traditional Sardinian flavors**. Some must-try dishes include **bottarga pasta, fregola with clams, malloreddus (Sardinian gnocchi), and porceddu (roast suckling pig)**. The region is also known for producing excellent wines, particularly **Vernaccia di Oristano**, a **golden-hued, fortified wine** with a **nutty, complex flavor**, which pairs beautifully with traditional Sardinian desserts such as **sebadas (honey-drizzled pastry filled with cheese)**.

Oristano offers a variety of **accommodation options**, ranging from **charming boutique hotels and agriturismi (farm stays) to budget-friendly guesthouses and seaside resorts**. Staying in the city center allows easy access to its historic attractions and vibrant local markets, while those looking for a more tranquil retreat can opt for accommodations near the **coastal areas of the Sinis Peninsula**.

The best time to visit Oristano depends on **travel preferences and activities**. The **spring and autumn months (April to June, September to October) offer pleasant weather, fewer crowds, and excellent conditions for sightseeing and outdoor activities**. **Summer (July to August)** is ideal for beach lovers, but it is also the busiest period, with higher temperatures and more visitors. **Winter (November to March)** is quieter, with mild temperatures and fewer tourists, making it a good time to explore historical sites and experience the Sartiglia festival in February.

Oristano is a hidden gem that showcases Sardinia's deep history, stunning landscapes, and rich cultural traditions. Whether wandering through its historic streets, witnessing the excitement of the Sartiglia, exploring ancient ruins, or relaxing on the spectacular beaches of the Sinis Peninsula, visitors will find a destination that combines authentic Sardinian charm with breathtaking natural beauty. It is an ideal place for travelers looking to experience history, nature, and tradition in a more tranquil and less touristy setting.

Olbia

Olbia, located on the **northeastern coast of Sardinia**, is one of the island's most important cities and serves as a major gateway for visitors arriving by air or sea. Known for its **bustling port, rich history, and proximity to the stunning beaches of Costa Smeralda**, Olbia is a dynamic city that offers a blend of **ancient archaeological sites, vibrant nightlife, excellent cuisine, and access to some of the most luxurious coastal resorts in the Mediterranean**. Although often viewed as a transit hub, Olbia is a destination in its own right, offering visitors a chance to explore **historic landmarks, cultural sites, and pristine natural beauty**.

Reaching Olbia is **quick and convenient**, as it is home to **Olbia Costa Smeralda Airport (OLB)**, which serves as one of Sardinia's busiest airports. The airport offers frequent **domestic flights from Rome, Milan, Venice, and Naples**, as well as **international connections to major European cities**, including **London, Paris, Berlin, Amsterdam, and Madrid**. From the airport, travelers can reach the city center in **about 10 minutes** by **bus, taxi, or** rental car. Olbia also has a **major ferry port**, with ferries arriving daily from **mainland Italy, including Genoa, Livorno, and Civitavecchia**, making it an essential arrival point for those traveling by sea. The city is well connected by road, with the **SS131 highway** linking Olbia to **Sassari and Alghero** and the **SS125 scenic coastal road** providing access to the Costa Smeralda and other northern destinations.

One of Olbia's most significant attractions is the **Basilica di San Simplicio, a beautiful Romanesque church dating back to the 11th century**. Built from granite, this historic structure is the most important religious monument in Olbia and a fine example of **medieval Sardinian architecture**. Inside, visitors can admire **ancient frescoes, stone carvings, and an underground crypt** that holds tombs from the early Christian period. Another notable landmark is the **Chiesa di San Paolo**, a striking **church with a colorful tiled dome**, located in the heart of Olbia's old town. The church's **Baroque interior and impressive facade** make it a must-visit site for history and architecture lovers.

Olbia's **historic center is lively and charming**, filled with **narrow streets, boutique shops, traditional restaurants, and open-air cafés**. The **Corso Umberto I**, the main street of the old town, is lined with **gelaterias, artisan stores, and bars**, making it the perfect place to stroll, shop, and enjoy local delicacies. The **Piazza Regina Margherita** is a bustling square where visitors can relax and take in the city's vibrant atmosphere, often accompanied by street performances and live music. The waterfront promenade, known as the **Lungomare**, offers **scenic views of the harbor, luxury yachts, and the nearby Tavolara Island**, making it an excellent spot for a sunset walk.

For those interested in Olbia's ancient past, the **Museo Archeologico di Olbia** provides fascinating insights into the city's **Phoenician, Greek, Roman, and medieval history**. The museum, located on **Peddone Island near the port**, showcases **Roman shipwrecks, ancient artifacts, and relics from Olbia's early settlements**. The **ruins of the Punic-Roman walls**, located near the museum, give further evidence of Olbia's importance as a strategic port city in antiquity. Another fascinating historical site is the **Sacred Well of Sa Testa**, an **ancient Nuragic water temple** located just outside the city, which dates back over **3,000 years** and is a testament to Sardinia's prehistoric civilization.

Olbia is surrounded by some of **Sardinia's most beautiful beaches**, making it a great base for exploring the region's stunning coastline. Just a short drive from the city, visitors can find **Pittulongu Beach**, a long stretch of **soft white sand and crystal-clear waters**, popular with both locals and tourists. The beach offers **beach clubs, sunbeds, and restaurants**, making it ideal for a relaxing day by the sea. Further north, **Spiaggia Bianca, Porto Istana, and Cala Sassari** offer **turquoise waters and picturesque landscapes**, perfect for swimming, snorkeling, and sunbathing. The nearby **Marinella Beach**, close to Porto Rotondo, is another spectacular spot known for its **shallow waters and fine sand**, making it great for families and water sports enthusiasts.

One of the most breathtaking natural sites near Olbia is the **Tavolara Island**, a dramatic **limestone massif rising from the sea**, just a short boat ride from the city. The island is part of a **marine protected area** and offers **hiking trails, snorkeling spots, and pristine beaches**, making it an excellent day-trip destination. Boat tours to Tavolara often include stops at **Molara Island and Cala Girgolu**, where visitors can discover **hidden coves, crystal-clear lagoons, and ancient rock formations**, such as the famous **Turtle Rock**. The **Capo Ceraso Nature Reserve**, located just south of Olbia, is another beautiful area offering **secluded beaches, hiking paths, and stunning coastal views**.

For luxury and glamour, visitors can take a short drive to the **Costa Smeralda**, one of the most exclusive destinations in the Mediterranean. Just **30 minutes from Olbia**, Costa Smeralda is famous for its **luxury resorts, designer boutiques, yacht-filled marinas, and stunning beaches**. The **prestigious town of Porto Cervo**, known for its high-end hotels, fine dining, and vibrant nightlife, attracts celebrities and elite travelers from around the world. The area is also home to **world-class golf courses, private beach clubs, and annual sailing regattas**, making it a playground for the rich and famous.

Olbia's **culinary scene** reflects the best of **Sardinian and Mediterranean cuisine**, with a strong emphasis on **fresh seafood, local produce, and traditional flavors**. Visitors should try **zuppa gallurese**, a rustic dish made with layers of **bread, pecorino cheese, and lamb broth**, which originates from the **Gallura region**. **Spaghetti with bottarga**, made with cured mullet roe, is another local specialty, while **fregola with clams**, a Sardinian **semolina pasta dish**, is a must-try for seafood lovers. The city is also known for its excellent wines, particularly **Vermentino di Gallura**, a **crisp and aromatic white wine** that pairs perfectly with seafood and light Mediterranean dishes. Restaurants along the **Lungomare and Corso Umberto I** offer a mix of **fine dining, traditional trattorias, and casual pizzerias**, catering to a wide range of tastes and budgets.

Olbia hosts **numerous festivals and cultural events** throughout the year, celebrating its **rich history, religious traditions, and local gastronomy**. One of the most important events is the **Feast of San Simplicio**, held every **May**, which honors the city's patron saint with **processions, concerts, fireworks, and traditional folk performances**. The **Autunno in Barbagia festival**, which takes place in the surrounding Gallura region during the fall, offers visitors a chance to experience **Sardinia's rural traditions, artisanal crafts, and authentic cuisine**.

Accommodation options in Olbia range from **luxury hotels and beachfront resorts to budget-friendly B&Bs and boutique guesthouses**. Upscale hotels such as **The Pelican Beach Resort** and **Geovillage Sport & Wellness Resort** offer **high-end amenities, spas, and stunning sea views**, while smaller guesthouses in the old town provide a more **intimate and authentic Sardinian experience**. For travelers looking to explore the **coastline and surrounding islands, vacation rentals and seaside villas** in nearby areas such as Pittulongu, Porto Rotondo, and San Teodoro provide excellent alternatives.

The best time to visit Olbia depends on travel preferences. **Spring (April to June) and autumn (September to October)** offer **pleasant temperatures, fewer crowds, and perfect conditions for sightseeing and outdoor activities**. **Summer (July to August)** is peak season, with **hot weather, lively nightlife, and bustling beaches**, while **winter (November to March)** is quieter, making it ideal for a more relaxed and cultural experience.

Olbia is a city that combines history, nature, and modern luxury, making it an ideal destination for travelers looking to experience authentic Sardinian culture alongside breathtaking coastal beauty. Whether exploring its ancient sites, relaxing on pristine beaches, or indulging in world-class cuisine, Olbia offers an unforgettable gateway to Sardinia's most spectacular landscapes and traditions.

CHAPTER 4: ATTRACTIONS

Ancient Nuraghe Sites: Barumini & More

Ancient Nuraghe sites are among the most fascinating and mysterious landmarks in Sardinia, offering a glimpse into the island's prehistoric past. These stone structures, built by the Nuragic civilization between 1800 and 400 BCE, are unique to Sardinia and continue to intrigue archaeologists and visitors alike. The Nuraghe of Barumini, known as Su Nuraxi di Barumini, is the most famous and well-preserved of all the Nuragic sites and has been designated a UNESCO World Heritage Site. However, beyond Barumini, Sardinia is home to thousands of Nuraghi, scattered across the island, each offering a unique perspective on this ancient culture. Visiting these sites allows travelers to step back in time and explore a civilization that thrived on the island long before the rise of the Roman Empire.

Barumini is located in south-central Sardinia, approximately 60 kilometers north of Cagliari, making it an easily accessible day trip from the capital. The site is best reached by car via the SS131 and SS197 highways, with a drive time of about one hour from Cagliari. Public transport options are available but limited, with buses running from Cagliari to Barumini on a less frequent schedule. Once in Barumini, visitors will find the Su Nuraxi archaeological site, which consists of a central Nuraghe tower surrounded by a complex system of defensive walls and ancient stone dwellings. This multi-layered settlement showcases the architectural evolution of the Nuragic civilization, with evidence of continued habitation from the Bronze Age to the Roman era.

Guided tours are required to explore the inner chambers, towers, and passageways of Su Nuraxi, providing visitors with an in-depth understanding of the site's historical significance. Archaeologists believe that the Nuraghi served as fortresses, religious centers, and communal dwellings, though their exact purpose remains debated. The main tower, originally over 18 meters high, offers breathtaking views of the surrounding Sardinian countryside and allows visitors to appreciate the engineering skill of the Nuragic people. Exploring the narrow stone corridors, spiral staircases, and defensive towers, visitors get a sense of how life may have been structured within these prehistoric settlements.

The Su Nuraxi complex is open daily, with operating hours varying seasonally. From April to October, the site is open from 9:00 AM to 7:30 PM, while from November to March, it operates on a reduced schedule from 9:00 AM to 5:00 PM. The entry fee for Su Nuraxi is approximately €14 per person, with discounts available for students, seniors, and children. Combination tickets can be purchased to include access to the Casa Zapata Museum, a historic Spanish palace in Barumini that houses additional Nuragic artifacts, and the Centro Giovanni Lilliu, a cultural center dedicated to the archaeologist who led the excavation of Su Nuraxi.

Beyond Barumini, Sardinia is home to numerous other Nuragic sites, each offering unique features and historical significance. One of the largest and most impressive is Nuraghe Santu Antine, located in the province of Sassari near Torralba. Often referred to as the "Nuragic Palace", this site features massive stone walls, interconnected chambers, and an advanced water drainage system, suggesting a highly organized and sophisticated society. Unlike Su Nuraxi, which was primarily a fortified settlement, Santu Antine is thought to have functioned as an administrative or ceremonial center. The central tower at Santu Antine, standing at over 17 meters tall, is one of the best-preserved examples of Nuragic engineering and provides a fascinating insight into Sardinia's prehistoric past.

Further north, near Arzachena in the Gallura region, visitors can explore Nuraghe Albucciu, a distinctive oval-shaped Nuraghe that blends into the surrounding rocky landscape. This site is unique due to its partially megalithic construction, incorporating natural rock formations into its defensive walls. Nearby, the Tomba dei Giganti (Tombs of the Giants) at Coddu Vecchiu and Li Lolghi showcase the funerary customs of the Nuragic people, with large stone structures that were believed to house collective burials. These impressive tombs, often over 10 meters long, suggest a society that placed great importance on ancestor worship and communal rites.

On the west coast near Oristano, the Nuraghe Losa, located close to Abbasanta, is another well-preserved site, notable for its trilobed structure and thick stone walls. Unlike Su Nuraxi, which was built with rough-hewn stones, Losa is constructed using precisely cut basalt blocks, demonstrating a more advanced building technique. The site also features remnants of a Nuragic village, defensive walls, and nearby sacred wells, highlighting the complexity of these ancient settlements.

The Sacred Well of Santa Cristina, located in the Oristano province, is one of the most mysterious and beautifully preserved Nuragic sites. This perfectly symmetrical well temple, built around 1200 BCE, is thought to have been used for rituals related to water worship and astronomy. During the equinox, sunlight aligns perfectly with the well's entrance, suggesting that the Nuragic people had an advanced understanding of celestial movements. The precision-cut basalt stones used in its construction, along with the well's remarkable state of preservation, make it one of the most awe-inspiring ancient structures in Sardinia.

Visiting multiple Nuragic sites allows travelers to understand the diversity of the Nuragic civilization, from fortresses and settlements to sacred temples and burial structures. Most sites offer guided tours, with entry fees ranging from €5 to €12, depending on the location. Some sites, such as Su Nuraxi and Nuraghe Santu Antine, require guided access for safety and preservation reasons, while others, like the Tombs of the Giants and Santa Cristina, can be explored independently.

For travelers looking to immerse themselves in Sardinia's prehistoric past, planning a Nuragic road trip is an excellent way to experience these ancient wonders. Renting a car is the best option, as many of the sites are located in rural areas with limited public transportation options. Visitors can combine their Nuragic exploration with visits to nearby villages, traditional Sardinian agriturismi, and local museums to gain a deeper appreciation for the island's ancient and modern culture.

The best time to visit Sardinia's Nuragic sites is during the spring (April to June) and autumn (September to October) when temperatures are mild, and the landscape is at its most beautiful. Summer (July and August) can be very hot, especially when exploring open-air sites like Su Nuraxi, where shade is limited. Bringing comfortable walking shoes, sunscreen, and plenty of water is essential, as many of these locations involve walking on rocky terrain and uneven surfaces.

Exploring the ancient Nuraghe sites of Barumini and beyond provides a fascinating window into a mysterious civilization that left behind some of the most remarkable prehistoric architecture in Europe. From massive stone fortresses to sacred temples and burial sites, these landmarks tell the story of a complex and advanced society that flourished in Sardinia for over a thousand years. Whether visiting the iconic Su Nuraxi, the towering Santu Antine, or the mystical well of Santa Cristina, travelers will find themselves stepping into a world shrouded in mystery, engineering marvels, and a deep connection to the past. These sites remain some of Sardinia's most extraordinary and historically significant attractions, making them a must-visit for history lovers, archaeology enthusiasts, and curious travelers alike.

Spectacular Beaches: Spiaggia della Pelosa, Cala Luna & Costa Rei

Sardinia is home to some of the most breathtaking beaches in the Mediterranean, each offering a unique blend of turquoise waters, soft white sands, and stunning coastal landscapes. Among the island's most famous and picturesque beaches are Spiaggia della Pelosa in the northwest, Cala Luna on the eastern coast, and Costa Rei in the southeast. These beaches are widely regarded as some of the most beautiful in Italy, drawing visitors from around the world to experience their pristine beauty, crystal-clear waters, and diverse activities. Whether you're looking for a relaxing beach escape, an adventure-filled coastal trek, or a place to snorkel and explore marine life, these stunning beaches provide an unforgettable experience.

Spiaggia della Pelosa, located near Stintino in the northwestern part of Sardinia, is often considered one of the most iconic and visually stunning beaches in the Mediterranean. Famous for its shallow, transparent waters and fine white sand, it resembles a tropical paradise rather than a typical Mediterranean coastline. The beach is set against the backdrop of Asinara Island and the Torre della

Pelosa, a historic 16th-century watchtower that adds to the beach's unique and picturesque charm. Spiaggia della Pelosa is best accessed from Alghero or Sassari, with Stintino located approximately 50 kilometers from Alghero. Visitors traveling by car can take the SP34 coastal road, which offers spectacular views of the turquoise waters and surrounding coastline. Parking near the beach is available but can be limited during peak season, so arriving early in the morning is highly recommended.

To protect its delicate ecosystem, Spiaggia della Pelosa has strict regulations, including a requirement for visitors to use woven beach mats instead of towels to prevent sand erosion. During the summer months (June to September), visitor numbers are restricted, and an entry fee of approximately €3.50 per person is required to access the beach. Booking in advance through the official website is necessary to secure a spot. Despite these restrictions, the beach remains incredibly popular, and visitors can enjoy swimming, snorkeling, and paddleboarding in the shallow, crystal-clear waters. The area surrounding Spiaggia della Pelosa also offers a variety of restaurants, cafés, and seafood trattorias, making it easy for visitors to enjoy fresh Sardinian cuisine after a day by the sea. The best time to visit is during the shoulder seasons of May to early June and September to October, when the weather is warm, and the beach is less crowded.

On Sardinia's eastern coast, Cala Luna is one of the island's most dramatic and breathtaking beaches, famous for its golden sands, towering limestone cliffs, and large sea caves that provide shade and shelter from the sun. Cala

Luna is located in the Gulf of Orosei, a region known for its rugged coastline, hidden coves, and stunning hiking trails. The beach is only accessible by boat or on foot, adding to its remote and untouched beauty. Boat trips to Cala Luna depart from Cala Gonone, Arbatax, and Santa Maria Navarrese, with round-trip boat tickets costing between €20 and €40 per person, depending on the season and departure point. For those seeking a more adventurous approach, Cala Luna can also be reached by a challenging but rewarding 3-hour hike from Cala Fuili, passing through dense Mediterranean vegetation, limestone rock formations, and scenic viewpoints overlooking the sea.

Cala Luna's crystal-clear waters and rich marine life make it an ideal spot for snorkeling and diving, with underwater caves and coral formations waiting to be explored. The beach itself is known for its large grottoes, where visitors can find shade and enjoy the cool sea breeze while taking in the stunning landscape. The remote nature of Cala Luna means there are no major restaurants or beach clubs, so visitors should bring their own water, snacks, and sun protection. The best time to visit is between May and September, though arriving early in the morning ensures a more peaceful experience before the midday boats bring in more visitors. Cala Luna remains one of Sardinia's most unspoiled and picturesque beaches, perfect for those seeking a mix of adventure, relaxation, and natural beauty

On the southeastern coast of Sardinia, Costa Rei is known for its long stretches of golden sand, shallow turquoise waters, and stunning panoramic views. This beach is one of the most family-friendly destinations on the island, offering gentle waves, ample space, and a relaxed atmosphere. Costa Rei is located about 50 kilometers from Cagliari, making it an easily accessible beach destination for those staying in southern Sardinia. The drive from Cagliari follows the scenic coastal road SS125, which provides breathtaking views of the Mediterranean coastline, rolling hills, and crystal-clear waters.

Costa Rei is famous for its soft sand and warm, shallow waters, making it ideal for families with children, couples, and beachgoers looking for a peaceful escape. The beach stretches for nearly 10 kilometers, offering plenty of space for sunbathing, swimming, and water sports. Several beach clubs and resorts along the coastline provide sun loungers, umbrellas, and beachfront dining, making it convenient for visitors who want a more luxurious and comfortable beach experience. Unlike Spiaggia della Pelosa, Costa Rei does not have entry restrictions or fees, making it a freely accessible beach for all visitors.

One of the highlights of Costa Rei is Scoglio di Peppino, a famous granite rock formation located at the southern end of the beach. Visitors can climb the rock to enjoy a stunning panoramic view of the coastline and surrounding mountains. The beach is also a popular spot for snorkeling, kayaking, and paddleboarding, with calm and clear waters perfect for marine exploration. During the evening, Costa Rei transforms into a relaxed and charming beach town, with lively restaurants, open-air markets, and bars offering fresh seafood, local wines, and traditional Sardinian dishes. The best time to visit is during the late spring and early autumn months, when temperatures are warm, but crowds are smaller compared to the peak summer season.

Each of these beaches—Spiaggia della Pelosa, Cala Luna, and Costa Rei—offers a unique and unforgettable experience that showcases Sardinia's breathtaking natural beauty, crystal-clear waters, and pristine coastlines. Whether visitors are looking for a tropical-like paradise with strict environmental protections, an adventurous beach set against dramatic cliffs and sea caves, or a long stretch of golden sand perfect for a family retreat, these beaches represent the diverse and stunning coastal landscapes of Sardinia. With easy access from nearby cities, opportunities for snorkeling, hiking, and water sports, and a mix of relaxation and adventure, these beaches stand out as some of the most spectacular seaside destinations in the Mediterranean. Visitors planning a trip to Sardinia should make sure to include at least one of these beaches in their itinerary to fully experience the island's unparalleled coastal beauty and serene atmosphere.

Natural Wonders: Gola di Gorropu & Monte Arcosu

Gola di Gorropu Canyon and Monte Arcosu Reserve are two of Sardinia's most breathtaking natural wonders, offering visitors an opportunity to explore the island's untamed landscapes, diverse wildlife, and dramatic geological formations. These two destinations showcase the raw beauty and ecological richness of Sardinia, making them perfect for travelers who enjoy hiking, wildlife watching, and experiencing nature in its purest form. Both sites provide an immersive outdoor experience, from the towering limestone cliffs of Gorropu Canyon, one of the deepest gorges in Europe, to the lush, wildlife-filled forests of Monte Arcosu Reserve, a protected natural area teeming with rare and endemic species.

Gola di Gorropu, often referred to as "Europe's Grand Canyon", is a spectacular limestone gorge carved by the Flumineddu River, located in eastern Sardinia within the Supramonte mountain range. It lies between the municipalities of Urzulei and Orgosolo, approximately 110 kilometers south of Olbia and 90 kilometers north of Cagliari. The canyon is famous for its sheer rock walls that rise over 500 meters, creating a dramatic and otherworldly landscape that attracts hikers, climbers, and nature enthusiasts from around the world. The best way to reach Gorropu is by car, driving along the SS125 highway, one of Sardinia's most scenic roads, which winds through rugged mountains and breathtaking valleys. Visitors can park at the

Genna Silana Pass (1,017 meters above sea level), which serves as the main trailhead for hiking into the canyon.

The hike into Gorropu Canyon is one of the most rewarding yet challenging treks in Sardinia. The most common route starts from Genna Silana, covering approximately 12 kilometers round trip, descending through the oak and juniper forests of the Supramonte before reaching the entrance of the canyon. The hike takes around 2 to 3 hours one way, depending on fitness level, and involves rocky and uneven terrain. Along the way, visitors can admire the stunning mountain scenery, endemic plant species, and occasional sightings of Sardinian wildlife such as mouflons, golden eagles, and peregrine falcons. Once inside the canyon, hikers will find themselves surrounded by towering cliffs and narrow rock passages, with sections of the gorge becoming increasingly difficult to navigate due to large boulders and steep rock formations. There are different levels of difficulty within the canyon itself, with color-coded zones marking easy (green), moderate (yellow), and extreme (red) sections. The most challenging parts require technical climbing skills, and access beyond a certain point is restricted without a certified guide.

Gorropu Canyon is open year-round, but the best time to visit is during spring (April to June) and autumn (September to October) when temperatures are mild, and the landscape is lush and green. Summer (July and August) can be extremely hot, making the hike more strenuous, while winter (November to March) may bring occasional rainfall, making some paths slippery. The entrance fee to the canyon is approximately €5 to €10 per person, with additional costs for guided tours, which range from €30 to €50 per person depending on the package. There are no age restrictions for the easier trails, but younger children and elderly visitors should avoid the more technical sections of the canyon. Hikers should wear sturdy hiking boots, bring plenty of water, and carry snacks, as there are no facilities inside the gorge.

Monte Arcosu Reserve, located in southern Sardinia, about 25 kilometers from Cagliari, is a protected nature reserve covering over 4,000 hectares of mountainous and forested terrain. Managed by the WWF (World Wildlife Fund), it is one of Sardinia's most important conservation areas, home to the largest population of Sardinian deer, as well as wild boars, foxes, Sardinian wildcats, and numerous bird species. The reserve's dense forests, flowing streams, and rugged peaks provide a sanctuary for rare and endangered species, making it an ideal destination for wildlife lovers, hikers, and photographers. Monte Arcosu is best reached by car, taking the SS195 road from Cagliari towards Capoterra, with well-marked signs leading to the entrance.

Visitors to Monte Arcosu can choose from a variety of hiking trails, ranging from easy walks to more strenuous mountain treks. The most popular trail leads to the scenic summit of Monte Arcosu, offering panoramic views of the surrounding mountains, forests, and coastline. This moderate hike takes around 2 to 3 hours round trip and passes through Mediterranean scrubland, oak groves, and small waterfalls, providing plenty of opportunities to spot wildlife and native plant species. There are also shorter, family-friendly trails suitable for children and beginners, allowing visitors to explore the tranquil beauty of the reserve at a more relaxed pace.

Monte Arcosu is open to visitors from spring to autumn, with operating hours typically from 9:00 AM to 6:00 PM. Entry fees are around €5 to €10 per person, with discounts for children, students, and WWF members. Guided tours are available for those who want to learn more about the reserve's ecology, conservation efforts, and local wildlife, with tours costing between €20 and €40 per person depending on duration and group size. The reserve is ideal for families and nature enthusiasts of all ages, but certain steep and rocky trails may not be suitable for very young children or individuals with mobility issues.

One of the most unique experiences at Monte Arcosu is the opportunity to participate in wildlife tracking and conservation activities, where visitors can learn about WWF's efforts to protect the Sardinian deer and other endangered species. The reserve also hosts seasonal events, workshops, and educational programs, making it an excellent place for those interested in environmental conservation and sustainable tourism. Visitors are encouraged to bring binoculars for birdwatching, as Monte Arcosu is home to a variety of raptors, including Bonelli's eagles, buzzards, and kestrels.

Both Gola di Gorropu Canyon and Monte Arcosu Reserve provide an immersive experience in Sardinia's diverse landscapes, offering opportunities to explore deep canyons, dense forests, towering mountains, and untouched wilderness. While Gorropu is best suited for adventure seekers and experienced hikers, Monte Arcosu offers a more tranquil and family-friendly environment, ideal for those who want to observe wildlife and enjoy nature at a slower pace. Whether trekking through one of the deepest canyons in Europe or exploring a conservation reserve filled with rare species, visitors to these sites will experience some of the most breathtaking and ecologically rich areas in Sardinia, making them unmissable destinations for nature lovers and outdoor enthusiasts.

Landmarks: Roman Amphitheaters, Cathedrals & Towers

Among the most significant historical landmarks on the island are its Roman amphitheaters, grand cathedrals, and medieval towers, each telling a unique story about Sardinia's past. These structures stand as remarkable testaments to the island's architectural and cultural evolution, attracting history enthusiasts, architecture lovers, and curious travelers alike. Visitors can walk through ancient Roman arenas, marvel at intricately decorated cathedrals, and climb medieval towers that once served as defensive strongholds against invaders. Whether exploring the remains of the Roman Amphitheater of Cagliari, admiring the grandeur of Cattedrale di Santa Maria in Alghero, or standing atop the Torre dell'Elefante, these sites provide an unforgettable journey through Sardinia's historical past.

The Roman Amphitheater of Cagliari is one of the island's most impressive ancient structures, showcasing the influence of the Roman Empire on Sardinia. Located in Cagliari, the capital city of Sardinia, this amphitheater dates back to the 2nd century AD and was once the primary venue for gladiator battles, theatrical performances, and public executions. Unlike many Roman amphitheaters that were constructed with bricks and mortar, the one in Cagliari was carved directly into the limestone rock of the city's hills, giving it a unique and striking appearance. The site is easily accessible from the city center, located just a short walk from Piazza Yenne or Via Sant'Ignazio da Laconi. Visitors can explore the remains of the seating area, underground tunnels, and sections of the stage, where gladiators and wild animals once battled for the entertainment of Roman citizens. The amphitheater is open daily, with operating hours typically from 9:00 AM to 7:00 PM during peak tourist seasons, and reduced hours during winter. Entry fees are around €6 per person, with discounts available for students and seniors. Guided tours are available for an additional cost, providing deeper insights into the construction, use, and historical significance of the amphitheater. There are no strict age restrictions, making it an excellent site for families, although visitors should wear comfortable walking shoes due to uneven terrain.

Another remarkable Roman site is the Amphitheater of Nora, located in the ancient city of Nora, near Pula, about 40 kilometers southwest of Cagliari. Nora was one of the earliest Phoenician settlements in Sardinia and later became an important Roman town. The amphitheater, which overlooks the blue waters of the Mediterranean, once hosted performances, social gatherings, and political events. Today, it remains a well-preserved structure, surrounded by Roman baths, mosaics, and ruins of ancient temples, providing visitors with a fascinating look at the daily life of a Roman colony. The site is accessible by car or bus from Cagliari, and it is best visited during the spring and autumn months when temperatures are mild. Entry fees for the entire Nora archaeological site range from €7 to €10 per person, with guided tours available. Visitors of all ages are welcome, though exploring some of the ancient stone paths may require caution.

Among Sardinia's most beautiful and historically significant religious landmarks is the Cattedrale di Santa Maria in Cagliari, also known as Cagliari Cathedral. Situated in the historic Castello district, this cathedral was originally built in the 13th century by the Pisans and later underwent several modifications, blending Romanesque, Gothic, and Baroque architectural styles. Its grand facade, intricate carvings, and towering bell towers make it one of the most striking landmarks in the city. Inside, visitors can admire stunning frescoes, marble chapels, and an impressive crypt that houses the tombs of Pisan and Aragonese nobles. The cathedral is open daily, usually from 8:00 AM to 7:00 PM, with free entry, though donations are appreciated. Guided tours are available, offering deeper insights into the cathedral's artistic and historical significance. It is an accessible site for visitors of all ages, and its location in the Castello district provides the opportunity to explore other historical sites nearby, including the Bastione di Saint Remy and Torre di San Pancrazio.

Another stunning cathedral is the Cattedrale di Santa Maria in Alghero, also known as the Alghero Cathedral. This impressive structure, located in the historic center of Alghero, showcases a mix of Catalan-Gothic, Renaissance, and Baroque influences, reflecting the city's Spanish heritage. Construction began in the 16th century, and the cathedral remains one of the most important religious sites in Sardinia. The highlight of the cathedral is its octagonal bell tower, which offers panoramic views of Alghero's old town and the Mediterranean coastline. Visitors can also admire elaborate chapels, marble altars, and religious artwork that decorate the cathedral's interior. It is open daily, with visiting hours from 9:00 AM to 6:30 PM, and entrance is usually free, although a small fee may be required to climb the bell tower. Due to its central location in Alghero, it is easily accessible on foot from the main piazzas and waterfront promenade.

Sardinia's medieval towers also serve as important historical landmarks, originally built to defend the island from pirate attacks and foreign invasions. One of the most famous is the Torre dell'Elefante, located in Cagliari's Castello district. Constructed in 1307 by the Pisans, this tower was one of the main defensive structures protecting the city. It gets its name from the small stone elephant sculpture carved into its walls. Visitors can climb to the top of the tower, where they are rewarded with breathtaking views of Cagliari, the harbor, and the surrounding coastline. The tower is open for visitors during daylight hours, typically from 9:30 AM to 7:00 PM, and entrance fees range from €3 to €5 per person. There are no age restrictions, but the climb involves steep staircases, so it may not be suitable for those with mobility difficulties.

Another notable tower is the Torre di San Pancrazio, also located in Cagliari's Castello district. Built around the same time as Torre dell'Elefante, this tower was constructed to fortify the city against attacks. Like its counterpart, it provides spectacular views of the city and sea, and visitors can explore its stone walls, narrow passageways, and defensive features. Entry fees and hours are similar to those of Torre dell'Elefante, and visitors are encouraged to explore both towers when touring the historic district.

On the northwestern coast of Sardinia, near Stintino, stands the Torre della Pelosa, a small yet significant watchtower built in the 16th century by the Spanish to protect the coastline from pirate invasions. It is situated on a small islet near Spiaggia della Pelosa, one of Sardinia's most famous beaches. While the tower itself is not open for interior visits, it remains a symbolic landmark that adds to the beauty of the surrounding landscape. Visitors can admire it from the shore or paddle out on a kayak to get a closer view.

Sardinia's Roman amphitheaters, cathedrals, and towers are among the island's most fascinating historical sites, offering a glimpse into its ancient, medieval, and colonial past. From the grand Roman arenas that once hosted gladiator battles to the majestic cathedrals reflecting centuries of artistic influence, and the defensive towers that guarded the island against invaders, these landmarks provide a rich and immersive experience. Whether exploring the ruins of Cagliari's Roman Amphitheater, climbing the Torre dell'Elefante, or admiring the Alghero Cathedral, visitors will be captivated by Sardinia's deep-rooted history and architectural splendor.

CHAPTER 5: ACCOMMODATION

Hotels & Resorts

Sardinia is home to some of the most luxurious and exclusive hotels and resorts in the Mediterranean, offering visitors the chance to experience world-class hospitality, breathtaking coastal views, and high-end amenities in stunning surroundings. Whether travelers are looking for a secluded beachfront retreat, a five-star resort with spa services, or an opulent hotel in a historic city, Sardinia's luxury accommodations provide unparalleled comfort, fine dining, and top-tier experiences. Many of these high-end hotels and resorts are located in Costa Smeralda, Porto Cervo, Alghero, Cagliari, and the south coast, each offering distinct landscapes, elegant accommodations, and exceptional service. From lavish beachfront villas to stunning mountain retreats, Sardinia's luxury hotels and resorts cater to discerning travelers, honeymooners, celebrities, and families looking for the ultimate Mediterranean escape.

One of the most exclusive and iconic luxury resorts in Sardinia is Hotel Cala di Volpe, a Luxury Collection Hotel, located in Porto Cervo, Costa Smeralda. This world-famous five-star resort is set on one of the most beautiful stretches of coastline in the Mediterranean, offering guests breathtaking sea views, white-sand beaches, and high-end facilities. Designed to resemble a traditional Mediterranean fishing village, the hotel features rustic-chic architecture, pastel-colored facades, and charming terraces, blending luxury with authenticity. Guests can enjoy private beach access, an Olympic-sized saltwater pool, a state-of-the-art wellness center, and an on-site Michelin-starred restaurant serving gourmet Sardinian cuisine. The resort also offers private yacht rentals, golf courses, and helicopter transfers, making it a favorite among international celebrities and high-profile travelers. The check-in time at Hotel Cala di Volpe is typically from 3:00 PM, and check-out is by 12:00 PM. Room rates vary significantly based on the season, with average prices ranging from €1,200 to €5,000 per night during peak summer months. The resort welcomes guests of all ages, with special family-friendly services available, including kids' clubs and babysitting options.

Another premier luxury destination is Romazzino, a Belmond Hotel, Costa Smeralda, also located in the exclusive Porto Cervo area. This elegant resort offers luxurious rooms, suites, and private villas, all designed with whitewashed walls, handcrafted furniture, and panoramic terraces overlooking the turquoise waters of the Mediterranean. Guests staying at Romazzino can indulge in personalized spa treatments, exclusive beach access, a saltwater infinity pool, and world-class dining options featuring the finest Italian and Sardinian delicacies. The hotel's fitness center, tennis courts, and private yacht excursions provide plenty of recreational activities for those looking to explore the stunning Costa Smeralda coastline. Check-in at Romazzino is from 3:00 PM, with check-out by 12:00 PM. The average cost per night ranges from €900 to over €4,500, depending on the season and room type. The resort is family-friendly, offering children's activities, a kids' club, and family excursions while also catering to honeymooners and couples looking for a romantic getaway.

For travelers seeking a luxurious city stay with a mix of history and modern elegance, Palazzo Doglio in Cagliari is an excellent choice. Located in the heart of Sardinia's capital, this five-star boutique hotel combines timeless architecture with contemporary sophistication. Guests can enjoy spacious suites, fine dining at award-winning restaurants, a luxury spa, and proximity to Cagliari's top cultural attractions, including the Castello district and Poetto Beach. The hotel's interior courtyard, adorned with fountains and lush greenery, creates an oasis of tranquility in the middle of the bustling city. Palazzo Doglio offers private chauffeur services, exclusive wine-tasting experiences, and curated cultural tours, making it ideal for travelers looking to experience both luxury and authentic Sardinian heritage. Check-in time is from 3:00 PM, and check-out is by 11:00 AM. Room rates range from €300 to €1,500 per night, depending on the suite and season. The hotel is suitable for both families and couples, with child-friendly amenities available upon request.

On Sardinia's northwestern coast, Villa Las Tronas Hotel & Spa in Alghero is a historic luxury retreat offering breathtaking sea views, a private coastal location, and a blend of vintage charm and modern comforts. Once a royal residence, this exquisite five-star property features elegant suites, an infinity-edge pool overlooking the Mediterranean, a private beach, and a world-class wellness center with sea-view spa treatments. Guests can enjoy gourmet dining, sunset aperitivos on the terrace, and personalized boat excursions to the stunning coves of the Alghero coastline. The hotel's secluded setting makes it an ideal destination for romantic getaways, honeymooners, and those seeking an exclusive, intimate retreat. Check-in is from 3:00 PM, and check-out is by 11:00 AM. The average price per night starts at €500 and can go up to €2,500 for the most luxurious suites. Villa Las Tronas primarily caters to adult guests, making it a preferred choice for those looking for a tranquil, child-free escape.

For those who prefer a private luxury villa experience, Forte Village Resort, located near Santa Margherita di Pula on Sardinia's southern coast, is one of the most comprehensive five-star beachfront resorts in Europe. Spread across a beautiful, lush estate, the resort offers private bungalows, beachfront suites, and fully serviced villas with personal pools, direct beach access, and dedicated concierge services. Forte Village is known for its extensive range of activities, including a world-class spa, multiple swimming pools, a tennis academy, and water sports such as sailing, diving, and windsurfing. The resort also features a Michelin-starred restaurant, luxury shopping boutiques, and evening entertainment, ensuring guests experience a perfect blend of relaxation and excitement. It is particularly well-suited for families, with kid-friendly clubs, entertainment programs, and supervised activities. Check-in starts at 2:00 PM, and check-out is by 11:00 AM. Prices vary widely, from €600 per night for premium suites to over €10,000 per night for exclusive beachfront villas.

For a luxury eco-retreat, Petra Segreta Resort & Spa, located in the hills of San Pantaleo, offers a tranquil hideaway with panoramic views of the Costa Smeralda coastline. This five-star boutique resort combines rustic elegance with modern luxury, offering stone-built suites, infinity pools, a world-class spa, and a renowned gourmet restaurant serving organic farm-to-table cuisine. Surrounded by oak forests and granite rock formations, it provides the perfect setting for yoga retreats, holistic wellness programs, and nature lovers looking to explore Sardinia's inland beauty. Check-in begins at 3:00 PM, and check-out is by 12:00 PM. Prices start from €400 per night and can exceed €3,500 per night for private villas with infinity pools. The resort is primarily designed for adults and couples, offering a peaceful, romantic escape.

Luxury hotels and resorts in Sardinia offer an unparalleled level of comfort, elegance, and world-class services, whether set against the pristine beaches of Costa Smeralda, the historic streets of Cagliari, or the secluded landscapes of Alghero and Pula. These accommodations cater to high-end travelers, families, honeymooners, and those seeking relaxation in an exclusive setting, ensuring a truly unforgettable experience in one of the most beautiful and prestigious destinations in the Mediterranean.

Budget Stays & Camping

The island also offers a wide range of budget-friendly hostels and camping sites that allow travelers to experience its natural beauty and historic charm without breaking the bank. Whether visitors prefer staying in social and vibrant hostels in major cities like Cagliari, Alghero, and Olbia or opting for a nature-filled escape in well-equipped campgrounds near Sardinia's most scenic coastal areas and national parks, there are plenty of affordable options. Budget-friendly accommodations provide a comfortable stay with essential amenities, communal spaces for meeting fellow travelers, and access to some of Sardinia's most stunning locations, making them an ideal choice for backpackers, solo adventurers, and families on a budget.

One of the best budget hostels in Sardinia is Hostel Marina, located in the historic district of Cagliari, the island's capital. Set in a former monastery, this charming hostel blends history with modern comfort and offers spacious dormitories, private rooms, and a vibrant common area where travelers can socialize. The hostel is centrally located in Cagliari's Marina district, just a short walk from Piazza Yenne, the Bastione di Saint Remy, and Poetto Beach, making it a great base for exploring the city's main attractions. Travelers arriving by train or bus can reach the hostel in under 10 minutes from Cagliari's central station, while those arriving at Cagliari Elmas Airport can take a direct train or bus to the city center. Hostel Marina offers free Wi-Fi, a communal kitchen, 24-hour reception, and lockers for secure storage. The check-in time is typically from 2:00 PM, with check-out by 11:00 AM. Prices range from €20 to €35 per night for a dormitory bed and €50 to €80 for a private room, making it one of the most affordable stays in the city. There are no strict age restrictions, though guests under 18 must be accompanied by an adult.

For those looking for a hostel experience in northern Sardinia, B&B Alghero Hostel offers comfortable budget accommodations in the picturesque town of Alghero, known for its Catalan influences, historic old town, and stunning beaches. The hostel is located about 1.5 kilometers from the city center and 10 minutes from the beachfront promenade, making it easy to access both the lively town and the stunning coastline. Travelers arriving from Alghero-Fertilia Airport can take a direct bus to Alghero's city center, followed by a short walk or taxi ride to the hostel. The property features shared dorms, private rooms, free Wi-Fi, bike rentals, and a fully equipped kitchen for self-catering guests. Check-in starts at 3:00 PM, and check-out is by 10:30 AM. Dormitory beds cost between €25 and €40 per night, while private rooms range from €50 to €90, depending on the season. The hostel welcomes guests of all ages, though minors must be accompanied by a guardian.

Another excellent budget-friendly accommodation is Olbia City Hostel, located in the northeastern coastal town of Olbia, a major gateway to Costa Smeralda and nearby islands such as La Maddalena. This modern and well-maintained hostel provides affordable dormitory-style lodging, comfortable private rooms, and a welcoming atmosphere for budget-conscious travelers. The hostel is just a 15-minute walk from Olbia's historic center and a short bus ride from beaches such as Pittulongu and Porto Istana. The nearest airport, Olbia Costa Smeralda Airport, is only 5 kilometers away, making it an easy destination for international visitors. Amenities include free breakfast, a lounge area, an outdoor terrace, laundry services, and lockers for security. Check-in begins at 2:00 PM, and check-out is by 11:00 AM. Dormitory beds are available for €20 to €35 per night, while private rooms cost between €55 and €100 per night. The hostel has no major age restrictions, though young solo travelers under 18 may need parental consent.

For travelers who prefer camping under the stars, Sardinia offers several well-equipped and scenic camping sites, often located near the island's most beautiful beaches, forests, and mountains. One of the best options is Camping Village Laguna Blu, located just outside Alghero, along the northwestern coast of Sardinia. This well-maintained campsite is situated near Fertilia, only 10 minutes from Alghero's historic center and 5 minutes from Alghero-Fertilia Airport, making it one of the most convenient camping spots on the island. Travelers can reach the site by car, public bus, or bike, as it is well-connected to the main road network. The campsite offers tent pitches, mobile homes, and bungalows, making it suitable for both traditional campers and those looking for a more comfortable stay. Amenities include clean restrooms, hot showers, an on-site restaurant, a supermarket, a children's play area, and direct beach access. Check-in for camping spots starts at 12:00 PM, while bungalows and mobile homes can be checked into from 4:00 PM. Prices vary based on season, with tent pitches starting from €15 per night and mobile homes ranging from €60 to €150 per night. The campsite is family-friendly, welcoming guests of all ages.

Another fantastic camping option is Camping Capo Ferrato, located along Costa Rei, one of Sardinia's most beautiful beaches in the southeastern part of the island. This peaceful and scenic campground is perfect for nature lovers and beachgoers, offering direct access to the stunning turquoise waters and white sands of Costa Rei. The site is approximately 60 kilometers from Cagliari, with access via the scenic SS125 coastal road. Travelers can reach the campsite by car or public bus from Cagliari, with buses running frequently during the summer months. The campground provides tent pitches, camper van spaces, bungalows, and glamping tents with modern facilities such as hot showers, a mini-market, a restaurant serving local cuisine, and rental services for bikes and water sports equipment. Check-in starts at 12:00 PM for tent spaces and 3:00 PM for bungalows and mobile homes, with check-out required by 10:30 AM. Prices range from €12 per night for a basic tent pitch to €130 per night for a premium bungalow. The campsite is ideal for families, groups, and solo travelers, with no strict age restrictions.

For those seeking a more wilderness-focused camping experience, Camping Supramonte, located near Urzulei in the heart of Sardinia's Gennargentu National Park, offers an off-the-grid retreat surrounded by rugged mountains, hiking trails, and pristine landscapes. This campsite is best suited for adventurous travelers looking to explore Sardinia's inland natural beauty, including the famous Gola di Gorropu Canyon and Tiscali archaeological site. Due to its remote location, travelers are advised to arrive by car, following the SS125 highway to Urzulei. The campsite provides basic tent spaces, wooden cabins, shared restrooms, and a communal kitchen, ensuring a true back-to-nature experience. Check-in begins at 2:00 PM, and check-out is by 10:00 AM. Prices are extremely budget-friendly, with tent pitches starting at €10 per night and cabin rentals from €40 per night. This site is open to all ages, but families with small children should be aware that some hiking trails and activities may be challenging.

Sardinia's budget-friendly hostels and camping sites offer an excellent way to explore the island's breathtaking landscapes, historic cities, and stunning beaches without spending a fortune. Whether staying in a social hostel in Cagliari or Alghero, setting up a tent near the turquoise waters of Costa Rei, or experiencing a remote mountain retreat in Gennargentu National Park, budget-conscious travelers can find affordable and comfortable options suited to their adventure style and preferences.

Charming B&Bs & Agriturismi Stays

Among the best options for an immersive and warm stay are cozy bed & breakfasts and agriturismi, which provide comfortable lodgings, homemade Sardinian breakfasts, and a chance to connect with the island's traditions. Whether nestled in a historic city center, perched on a scenic hillside, or surrounded by olive groves and vineyards, these accommodations offer an intimate and welcoming atmosphere, perfect for couples, families, and solo travelers seeking a more personal and relaxed travel experience. Sardinia's bed & breakfasts (B&Bs) often provide stylish yet affordable stays in charming towns, while agriturismi (farm stays) allow guests to enjoy fresh, locally sourced food and rural tranquility.

One of the most charming bed & breakfasts in Cagliari is B&B Casa Marina, located in the historic Marina district, just a short walk from the bustling waterfront, the famous Bastione di Saint Remy, and Cagliari Cathedral. This beautifully decorated B&B combines modern comforts with traditional Sardinian aesthetics, featuring cozy rooms with private bathrooms, air conditioning, and a homemade breakfast each morning with freshly baked pastries, local honey, and strong Italian coffee. The B&B is conveniently located near Cagliari's central train station, making it easy for visitors arriving from Cagliari Elmas Airport via train or taxi. Check-in is available from 2:00 PM, and check-out is by 11:00 AM. Prices vary depending on the season, with rooms averaging €60 to €120 per night, including breakfast.

Casa Marina is an ideal choice for couples and solo travelers looking to experience Cagliari's vibrant culture, nightlife, and historical sites while enjoying a cozy and intimate accommodation.

For travelers looking to stay near Alghero, one of the most picturesque towns in northern Sardinia, B&B Alguer offers a charming retreat just steps from the medieval old town and Alghero's stunning seaside promenade. This small, family-run B&B is housed in a historic building with bright, airy rooms featuring local handcrafted decor, comfortable bedding, and private terraces with views of the Mediterranean Sea. Guests can enjoy a delicious Sardinian breakfast, including freshly made seadas (traditional honey-filled pastries), local cheeses, and fruit from nearby farms. The B&B is located about 10 minutes from Alghero-Fertilia Airport, with easy access by taxi or public bus. Check-in is from 3:00 PM, and check-out is by 11:00 AM. Prices range from €70 to €150 per night, depending on the season and room type. B&B Alguer is perfect for couples and families looking for a relaxing stay close to Alghero's beaches, shops, and restaurants.

For a more countryside experience, Sa Corti de Sa Perda in Costa Verde is a stunning B&B located in the unspoiled southwestern region of Sardinia, near Piscinas Beach and the wild sand dunes of Costa Verde. This rustic yet elegant guesthouse offers guests panoramic views of rolling hills, beautifully decorated stone-walled rooms, and an inviting garden with hammocks and a small pool. The hosts prepare a fresh daily breakfast featuring homemade cakes, jams, and farm-fresh eggs, providing an authentic taste of

Sardinian hospitality. Sa Corti de Sa Perda is best accessed by car from Cagliari or Oristano, as public transport options are limited in this remote area. Check-in is available from 2:30 PM, and check-out is by 10:30 AM. Room rates range from €55 to €110 per night, making it an excellent mid-range yet affordable option for those looking to explore Sardinia's wilder, less-touristy landscapes.

For those wanting an authentic agriturismo experience, Agriturismo Su Leunaxiu, located about 15 kilometers from Cagliari in the lush countryside of Soleminis, offers an immersive farm stay with locally sourced food and a peaceful rural atmosphere. This family-run agriturismo features traditional Sardinian-style rooms with wooden furnishings, large gardens, and farm animals, creating a tranquil escape from the city. The highlight of staying at Su Leunaxiu is the incredible homemade meals, prepared with farm-fresh ingredients, including homemade pasta, local meats, and fresh ricotta cheese. The agriturismo is easily accessible by car from Cagliari, with a drive of about 20 minutes along the SS387 road. Check-in starts at 3:00 PM, and check-out is by 11:00 AM. Room prices, including breakfast, range from €50 to €100 per night, while half-board and full-board meal options are available at an extra cost, typically around €25 to €35 per person for a full Sardinian dinner. This agriturismo is family-friendly, offering activities such as farm tours and cooking classes.

Another exceptional agriturismo is Tenuta Pilastru, located in the Gallura region, near Arzachena and Costa Smeralda. This agriturismo is set in the rolling countryside, surrounded by olive groves and cork oak forests, offering visitors a peaceful retreat just 20 minutes from some of Sardinia's most luxurious beaches. The property features rustic-chic stone bungalows, a wellness spa, and a restaurant serving farm-to-table Sardinian cuisine. Guests can enjoy activities such as wine tastings, horseback riding, and hiking through nearby nature trails, making it a great choice for nature lovers. The agriturismo is best reached by car, with Olbia Costa Smeralda Airport located about 30 kilometers away. Check-in is available from 2:30 PM, and check-out is by 11:00 AM. Prices for a double room with breakfast range from €90 to €180 per night, depending on the season, while dining options include traditional multi-course Sardinian meals for around €40 per person. Tenuta Pilastru is ideal for couples and families looking for a rural escape close to both nature and the glamour of Costa Smeralda.

For visitors exploring central Sardinia, Agriturismo Camisadu, located near Nuoro and the Supramonte mountains, provides a genuine farm-stay experience in one of the island's most rugged and traditional regions. This working farm produces organic vegetables, cheeses, and traditional Sardinian meats, which are served in delicious home-cooked meals featuring authentic recipes passed down for generations. The rooms are simple yet comfortable, reflecting Sardinia's pastoral heritage, with wooden ceilings and handcrafted furnishings. The agriturismo is accessible by car via the SS131 road, making it an ideal stop for those heading to Gorropu Canyon or the Orgosolo murals. Check-in starts at 3:00 PM, and check-out is by 10:30 AM. Prices range from €60 to €120 per night, with optional meals costing around €30 per person.

The property is family-friendly, offering agricultural workshops and guided nature walks, making it an excellent choice for travelers wanting a deeper connection with Sardinian traditions.

Sardinia's cozy bed & breakfasts and agriturismi provide warm hospitality, delicious food, and unique settings, whether nestled in the heart of a historic town, overlooking stunning coastal scenery, or set deep in the island's countryside. With affordable prices, personalized service, and a welcoming atmosphere, these accommodations allow travelers to experience the best of Sardinia without the crowds of large resorts or the cost of luxury hotels. Whether staying in a charming B&B in Alghero, a countryside farm in Gallura, or a traditional agriturismo near Nuoro, visitors will find a perfect blend of comfort, authenticity, and local charm, making their stay in Sardinia truly unforgettable.

CHAPTER 6: CUISINE AND DINING

Must-Try Sardinian Dishes

Sardinian cuisine is deeply rooted in the island's history, geography, and pastoral traditions, offering a unique and authentic experience that distinguishes it from mainland Italian food. Among the most iconic and must-try traditional Sardinian dishes are Porceddu (roast suckling pig), Culurgiones (stuffed pasta), and Pane Carasau (crispy flatbread). These dishes are not just food but symbols of Sardinia's rural heritage, centuries-old culinary techniques, and the island's deep respect for local ingredients. Whether dining in a traditional agriturismo in the Sardinian countryside, a family-run trattoria in Cagliari or Alghero, or a coastal seafood restaurant that incorporates these local delicacies, visitors will find that these dishes offer a genuine taste of Sardinia's rich cultural and gastronomic history.

One of the most famous and highly regarded dishes in Sardinia is Porceddu, a slow-roasted suckling pig that has been a staple of Sardinian feasts and celebrations for centuries. This dish is traditionally prepared using young piglets, no older than 40 days, which are seasoned with local herbs such as myrtle and rosemary before being slow-roasted on a spit over an open wood fire for several hours. The result is a crispy, golden skin encasing tender, flavorful meat, making it one of the most beloved dishes on the island. Porceddu is commonly served at agriturismi (farm stays) and traditional countryside restaurants, where it is cooked using age-old techniques to preserve its authenticity. Some of the best places to try Porceddu include Agriturismo Su Gologone near Oliena, Agriturismo Sa Mandra in Alghero, and Agriturismo Su Leunaxiu near Cagliari. These locations not only serve this delicacy in its most traditional form but also offer a complete immersive experience, allowing visitors to enjoy a rustic Sardinian feast, often accompanied by other local specialties such as roasted potatoes, seasonal vegetables, and Cannonau wine. The average cost of a Porceddu meal in an agriturismo ranges from €35 to €50 per person, usually as part of a multi-course dining experience. Given its labor-intensive preparation and cultural significance, trying Porceddu is a must for those who want to experience Sardinian hospitality and the island's traditional flavors at their best.

Another essential dish that visitors should not miss is Culurgiones, a type of handmade stuffed pasta that originates from the Ogliastra region in eastern Sardinia. Unlike traditional Italian ravioli, Culurgiones have a distinctive shape, resembling a wheat ear, symbolizing prosperity and good fortune. The pasta is filled with a rich and creamy mixture of potatoes, pecorino cheese, garlic, and fresh mint, creating a delicate yet flavorful balance that perfectly represents Sardinia's pastoral and agricultural roots. These dumplings are typically boiled and served with a simple tomato sauce, basil, and extra virgin olive oil, allowing their delicate flavors to shine. Some of the best places to enjoy authentic Culurgiones include Ristorante Da Concetta in Tortolì, Trattoria La Gritta in Cagliari, and

Antica Dimora del Gruccione in Santu Lussurgiu. These restaurants offer handmade Culurgiones prepared using traditional recipes passed down for generations. Prices for a plate of Culurgiones typically range from €12 to €18, depending on the location and whether it is served as part of a tasting menu. This dish is a must-try for pasta lovers because it embodies the simplicity and richness of Sardinian home cooking, reflecting the island's deep respect for high-quality ingredients and traditional techniques.

No traditional Sardinian meal is complete without Pane Carasau, a thin, crispy flatbread that has been a staple of Sardinian cuisine for centuries. Also known as "Carta da Musica" (sheet music bread) due to its delicate, paper-thin texture, Pane Carasau was originally created as a long-lasting bread for shepherds, who needed a food source that could withstand long journeys through the mountains. The bread is made by baking thin sheets of durum wheat dough at extremely high temperatures, causing them to puff up and separate into multiple layers. These layers are then sliced and baked again to achieve their signature crunchy texture. Pane Carasau is often served as an accompaniment to cheeses, cured meats, and soups, or drizzled with olive oil and sprinkled with salt for a simple yet delicious snack. It is also the base for Pane Frattau, a traditional dish where the crispy bread is layered with tomato sauce, pecorino cheese, and a poached egg, creating a savory and satisfying meal. Some of the best places to buy and taste freshly made Pane Carasau include Panificio Bulloni in Nuoro, Panificio Cherchi in Alghero, and Antico Forno Santa Chiara in Cagliari, where bakers still follow traditional methods of bread-making. For those dining in restaurants, Pane Carasau is commonly served as a complimentary appetizer or side dish, often paired with local cheeses such as Pecorino Sardo or Fiore Sardo. A package of freshly baked Pane Carasau can be purchased in Sardinian bakeries and specialty food stores for around €4 to €8, making it an excellent souvenir to take home.

Each of these traditional Sardinian dishes—Porceddu, Culurgiones, and Pane Carasau—offers a unique glimpse into the island's rich culinary traditions, showcasing the deep agricultural, pastoral, and gastronomic heritage that defines Sardinian cuisine. Whether enjoying a slow-cooked Porceddu feast in a rural agriturismo, savoring handmade Culurgiones in a family-run trattoria, or tasting the crisp texture of freshly baked Pane Carasau in a historic bakery, these dishes represent the soul of Sardinia's food culture. Visitors to Sardinia should not miss the opportunity to indulge in these flavors, as they encapsulate the island's history, craftsmanship, and dedication to preserving its culinary identity.

Fresh Seafood & Coastal Cuisine

Sardinia, surrounded by the pristine waters of the Mediterranean, is a paradise for seafood lovers, offering an array of fresh and flavorful seafood specialties that reflect the island's deep maritime traditions. Among the most beloved and distinctive seafood dishes are Bottarga (cured fish roe), Fregola ai Frutti di Mare (Sardinian couscous with seafood), and Grilled Fish (Pesce alla Griglia). These dishes capture the essence of Sardinian coastal cuisine, with their bold flavors, simple yet refined preparation, and reliance on high-quality, locally sourced ingredients. Whether dining in a beachfront trattoria in Alghero, a family-run seafood restaurant in Cagliari, or an upscale eatery along the Costa Smeralda, visitors will find these signature dishes on menus across the island, offering an unforgettable taste of Sardinia's culinary heritage.

One of the most iconic and prized seafood delicacies in Sardinia is Bottarga, a type of salted and cured fish roe, typically made from grey mullet (Bottarga di Muggine) or bluefin tuna (Bottarga di Tonno). Often referred to as "Sardinian caviar", Bottarga has a distinctive amber color, intense umami flavor, and a slightly briny, nutty taste, making it a favorite ingredient in traditional Sardinian cuisine. It is typically served grated over pasta, sliced thinly with olive oil and lemon, or paired with fresh bread and ricotta cheese. Some of the best places to experience Bottarga in Sardinia include Trattoria Gennargentu in Cagliari, Il Refettorio in Oristano, and Ristorante La Gritta in Palau, where chefs prepare Bottarga-based dishes using authentic local methods. The town of Cabras, located in the province of Oristano on the western coast, is considered the best place to purchase freshly made Bottarga, as it is home to some of the finest mullet fisheries in Sardinia. Visitors can find high-quality Bottarga in local markets and specialty food stores, such as Peschiera Pontis in Cabras or Rivamar in Cagliari, where they can sample and buy Bottarga to take home. The cost of Bottarga varies depending on quality and type, with whole dried roe sacs ranging from €50 to €120 per kilogram and pre-packaged grated Bottarga costing around €10 to €20 per jar. This delicacy is a must-try for seafood lovers because it offers a unique and concentrated taste of the sea, making it a versatile ingredient in Sardinian and Mediterranean cuisine.

Another beloved Sardinian seafood dish is Fregola ai Frutti di Mare, a traditional pasta dish made with small, toasted semolina pearls known as Fregola, cooked with a rich seafood sauce. Fregola is often compared to couscous, but its toasted preparation and slightly chewy texture make it unique to Sardinia. The dish is typically prepared with a mix of fresh seafood, including mussels, clams, prawns, and calamari, simmered in a flavorful tomato-based broth infused with garlic, white wine, saffron, and fresh herbs. The result is a deeply aromatic and satisfying dish that highlights the freshness of Sardinian seafood. Some of the best places to try Fregola ai Frutti di Mare include Sa Domu Sarda in Cagliari, Antica Trattoria La Saletta in Alghero, and Osteria del Mare in San Teodoro, where chefs use fresh, locally caught seafood to create an authentic and flavorful version of this dish. Many of these restaurants are located near fishing ports, ensuring that the seafood is as fresh as possible, often sourced the same day from local fishermen. The average price for a plate of Fregola ai Frutti di Mare ranges from €15 to €25, depending on the quality of the seafood used. This dish is a must-try for visitors wanting to experience a truly Sardinian take on seafood pasta, as it blends the island's agricultural and maritime traditions into one flavorful, comforting dish.

For those who appreciate simplicity and the natural flavors of the sea, Grilled Fish (Pesce alla Griglia) is a Sardinian specialty that showcases the island's freshest seafood with minimal seasoning and maximum flavor. Sardinia's coastal towns and fishing villages are known for their abundant supply of high-quality fish, including sea bass (spigola), bream (orata), red snapper (dentice), and swordfish (pesce spada), which are grilled whole or filleted over an open flame. The fish is typically seasoned only with sea salt, olive oil, and a squeeze of lemon, allowing its natural flavors to shine. Some of the best places to enjoy Grilled Fish in Sardinia include Ristorante Dal Corsaro in Cagliari, Al Tuguri in Alghero, and Trattoria al Porto in La Maddalena, all of which specialize in locally caught fish, expertly grilled and served with simple yet delicious accompaniments such as roasted potatoes, grilled vegetables, or fresh salads. Many of these restaurants are located near fishing harbors, where diners can watch boats bring in the day's catch, ensuring the freshest possible seafood on their plate. For visitors who prefer a more rustic and traditional experience, coastal agriturismi such as Agriturismo La Biada in Villasimius and Agriturismo La Locanda del Parco near Cala Gonone offer farm-to-table seafood dining experiences, where guests can enjoy grilled fish straight from the local fishermen's boats. The cost of a grilled fish dish varies depending on the type of fish and portion size, with prices ranging from €20 to €40 per dish. This dish is essential for seafood lovers because it embodies the essence of Mediterranean cuisine—fresh, simple, and expertly prepared to highlight the purity of the ingredients.

Each of these Sardinian seafood specialties—Bottarga, Fregola ai Frutti di Mare, and Grilled Fish—offers a distinct and memorable taste of the island's maritime traditions. Whether enjoying the salty, rich intensity of Bottarga, the hearty and comforting flavors of Fregola cooked with fresh shellfish, or the clean and delicate taste of fire-grilled fish, visitors will find that Sardinian seafood is among the best in the Mediterranean. These dishes can be enjoyed in seaside trattorias, upscale restaurants, or rustic agriturismi, each providing a unique and authentic experience that reflects Sardinia's deep connection to the sea and its culinary heritage. A trip to Sardinia is not complete without sampling these signature seafood specialties, which offer a true taste of the island's history, flavors, and dedication to high-quality, fresh ingredients.

Sweets & Desserts

Among the most iconic and must-try Sardinian desserts are Seadas, Amaretti, and Torrone, each offering a unique taste that showcases the island's dedication to time-honored recipes and quality ingredients. These traditional sweets can be found in local pastry shops, historic cafés, village festivals, and high-end restaurants across the island, making them an essential part of any culinary experience in Sardinia. Whether indulging in a warm, honey-drizzled Seada, savoring the almond-infused softness of Amaretti, or enjoying the crunchy, nut-filled texture of Sardinian Torrone, visitors will find that Sardinian desserts are deeply tied to the island's heritage and seasonal celebrations.

One of the most famous and beloved desserts in Sardinia is Seadas, a dish that perfectly balances sweet and savory flavors. Traditionally made with a thin, crispy semolina pastry filled with fresh pecorino cheese, Seadas are deep-fried until golden brown and drizzled generously with local honey, usually from wildflower, thyme, or eucalyptus varieties, adding a distinct floral and aromatic sweetness. This dessert dates back to Sardinia's pastoral traditions, when shepherds created simple yet delicious recipes using the ingredients they had on hand—cheese, flour, and honey. The cheese filling provides a slightly tangy contrast to the sweetness of the honey, creating a rich and satisfying dessert that is best eaten warm. Seadas are found in traditional trattorias, agriturismi, and pastry shops all over Sardinia, but some of the best places to try them include Trattoria Lillicu in Cagliari, Al Tuguri in Alghero, and

Antica Dimora del Gruccione in Santu Lussurgiu, where chefs prepare Seadas using authentic methods and locally sourced ingredients. Visitors can also purchase freshly made Seadas from artisan bakeries such as Pasticceria Puggioni in Nuoro or Panificio Cherchi in Sassari, where they can either enjoy them on-site or take them home to prepare later. The average cost for a serving of Seadas in a restaurant is between €5 and €8, while pre-packaged Seadas from a bakery can cost around €10 to €15 for a box of four. This dessert is a must-try because it is one of the most authentic representations of Sardinian culinary heritage, showcasing the island's love for high-quality cheese, honey, and traditional pastry-making techniques.

Another essential Sardinian sweet that visitors must try is Amaretti, a type of soft almond cookie that has been a part of Sardinian culinary tradition for centuries. Made with ground almonds, egg whites, and sugar, these chewy and aromatic cookies are known for their delicate balance of sweetness and nuttiness, often enhanced with a hint of lemon zest or bitter almonds. Unlike the harder Amaretti cookies found in other regions of Italy, Sardinian Amaretti are moist and tender, with a texture that melts in the mouth. These cookies are often served with coffee or sweet dessert wines, making them a perfect treat to enjoy after a meal or as an afternoon indulgence. Some of the best places to try handmade Amaretti include Pasticceria Mura in Oristano, Pasticceria Vanali in Alghero, and Dolci Sardi in Cagliari, all of which produce fresh, high-quality Amaretti using traditional methods and locally grown almonds. Visitors can also find Amaretti at local markets and specialty food shops, where they are often sold in beautifully wrapped packages, making them a perfect edible souvenir from Sardinia. The average price for a small bag of Amaretti cookies ranges from €5 to €12, depending on the quality and brand. This treat is a must-try for dessert lovers because it offers a delicious and authentic taste of Sardinia's almond-rich landscape, and its simple yet refined flavor pairs perfectly with coffee, tea, or a glass of Mirto liqueur.

For those who love crunchy, nutty confections, Sardinian Torrone is an absolute must-try. Torrone, a traditional nougat made with honey, egg whites, and toasted nuts such as almonds, hazelnuts, or walnuts, is a staple in Sardinian festivals, markets, and holiday celebrations. Unlike the classic Italian Torrone, which is often made with sugar and has a softer consistency, Sardinian Torrone is entirely sweetened with honey, giving it a richer, more aromatic flavor and a chewier, firmer texture. The town of Tonara, located in the Barbagia region, is considered the home of Sardinia's finest Torrone, with generations of families continuing the art of nougat-making using the island's best honey and nuts. Visitors to Tonara can visit local torronifici (nougat factories) such as Torronificio Tore, Torronificio Pruneddu, and Torronificio Pili, where they can watch the nougat being made by hand and sample different varieties, including classic almond Torrone, hazelnut Torrone, and honey-infused variations. For those unable to visit Tonara, high quality Torrone can also be found in specialty shops in Cagliari, Nuoro, and Sassari, such as Sa Torrera in Cagliari or Pasticceria Tettamanzi in Sassari. The cost of Sardinian Torrone ranges from €10 to €25 per kilogram, depending on the type and quality of the ingredients used.

This dessert is a must-try because it represents the heart of Sardinia's confectionery tradition, using local honey and nuts to create a treat that has been enjoyed for centuries, particularly during special occasions and family gatherings.

Each of these traditional Sardinian desserts—Seadas, Amaretti, and Torrone—offers a unique and delicious way to experience the island's sweet side. Whether indulging in the crispy, cheese-filled goodness of Seadas drizzled with honey, savoring the delicate almond-rich flavor of Amaretti, or enjoying the chewy, honey-sweetened crunch of Sardinian Torrone, visitors will find that Sardinia's sweets are as rich in history as they are in flavor. These treats can be found in bakeries, traditional restaurants, and local markets, making them easily accessible no matter where visitors choose to explore the island. A trip to Sardinia is incomplete without trying these iconic desserts, which showcase the island's deep-rooted culinary traditions, its use of high-quality local ingredients, and its passion for creating unforgettable flavors that have been passed down through generations.

Wines and Spirits

The island's unique terroir, characterized by its granite-rich soil, Mediterranean climate, and coastal breezes, produces wines and spirits with bold flavors and deep cultural significance. Among the most famous and must-try local beverages are Cannonau, Vermentino, and Mirto, each offering a distinctive taste that embodies the essence of Sardinian winemaking and traditional distillation techniques. Whether visiting a family-run vineyard in the rolling hills of Barbagia, sampling fresh Vermentino at a seaside enoteca in Alghero, or sipping homemade Mirto in a rustic agriturismo, experiencing these drinks is an essential part of discovering Sardinia's culinary and cultural heritage.

Cannonau di Sardegna is perhaps the most iconic red wine of Sardinia, renowned for its rich, full-bodied character and high antioxidant content. Made from the Cannonau grape, which is believed to be one of the oldest wine varieties in the Mediterranean, this red wine is known for its deep ruby color, bold tannins, and complex flavors of ripe red fruits, spices, and earthy undertones. The wine is often aged in oak barrels, adding hints of vanilla, tobacco, and balsamic notes that further enhance its depth. Cannonau is widely associated with Sardinia's longevity, as studies have linked the high levels of polyphenols in Cannonau to the island's high number of centenarians, particularly in Barbagia, where this wine is traditionally produced. Some of the best places to taste and purchase authentic Cannonau include Cantina Argiolas in Serdiana, Cantina Gabbas in Nuoro, and Cantina Giuseppe Sedilesu in Mamoiada, all of which specialize in crafting high-quality Cannonau using traditional winemaking methods. Visitors can tour these wineries, walk through the vineyards, and enjoy guided tastings that showcase different aging styles, from young, fresh Cannonau to aged Riserva wines with deeper complexity. Many restaurants and wine bars across Sardinia also serve top-quality Cannonau, with recommended stops including Vineria Tola in Alghero, Enoteca Vinoteca in Cagliari, and Il Cormorano in Castelsardo. The average cost for a bottle of Cannonau ranges from €12 to €35, depending on the producer and vintage, making it an affordable yet high-quality option for wine lovers. This wine is a must-try because it is deeply rooted in Sardinia's history, embodies the island's bold and rustic flavors, and pairs beautifully with traditional dishes such as roast lamb, Pecorino Sardo cheese, and hearty pasta dishes.

For those who prefer white wines, Vermentino di Gallura is the most celebrated white wine of Sardinia, known for its crisp, aromatic profile and refreshing minerality. Grown primarily in the Gallura region in northern Sardinia, where the granite-rich soils and warm coastal climate enhance its flavor profile, Vermentino is light-bodied yet complex, offering notes of citrus, green apple, white flowers, and a distinctive saline finish. It is one of the only DOCG wines in Sardinia, signifying its exceptional quality and strict production standards. This wine is the perfect companion for Sardinia's seafood cuisine, pairing excellently with grilled fish, shellfish, and Fregola ai Frutti di Mare. Some of the best wineries to visit for Vermentino tastings include Cantina Surrau in Arzachena, Tenuta Olbios near Olbia, and Vigne Surrau in Porto Cervo, where visitors can enjoy vineyard tours, wine tastings, and food pairings with local cheeses and seafood specialties. The best wine bars to sample Vermentino include La Bottega del Vermentino in Olbia, Osteria del Vino in Sassari, and Cagliari's Enoteca Vitis Vinifera, all of which offer a wide selection of Vermentino wines from different producers across Sardinia. The average price for a bottle of Vermentino ranges from €10 to €30, making it an accessible and refreshing option for those who appreciate high-quality white wines. This wine is a must-try because it captures the essence of Sardinia's coastal landscape, with its crisp acidity, vibrant aromas, and mineral-rich taste that perfectly complements the island's fresh seafood dishes.

For those seeking a true taste of Sardinian tradition, Mirto is the island's most famous and beloved liqueur, made from wild myrtle berries that grow abundantly across Sardinia's hills and coastal regions. This deep ruby-red liqueur is produced by macerating myrtle berries in alcohol, then blending it with honey or sugar to create a rich, aromatic digestivo. The flavor of Mirto is intensely herbal, slightly sweet, and deeply warming, making it the perfect after-dinner drink. Mirto comes in two main varieties: Mirto Rosso (red Mirto), made from ripe myrtle berries, and Mirto Bianco (white Mirto), made from myrtle leaves and unripe berries, resulting in a more delicate and aromatic profile. Some of the best places to try Mirto include historic distilleries such as Liquorificio Pacini in Cagliari, Distilleria Rau in Alghero, and Silvio Carta Distillery in Oristano, where visitors can tour the production facilities, learn about the distillation process, and taste different variations of Mirto. Many agriturismi and traditional restaurants also serve house-made Mirto, often crafted using family recipes passed down through generations, providing an authentic and artisanal experience. Some of the best places to enjoy locally made Mirto include Agriturismo Su Gologone near Oliena, Trattoria Sa Domu Sarda in Cagliari, and Ristorante Il Rifugio in Villasimius, where Mirto is served as a digestif after a hearty Sardinian meal. The cost of a bottle of Mirto ranges from €15 to €40, with artisanal and aged varieties being more expensive due to their longer maceration and higher-quality ingredients. Mirto is a must-try because it is a deeply traditional Sardinian spirit, offering a taste of the island's wild landscape in every sip, and it serves as the perfect way to end a meal with its smooth, aromatic, and slightly bitter-sweet finish.

Sardinia's local wines and spirits—Cannonau, Vermentino, and Mirto—each tell a unique story of the island's rich winemaking and distillation heritage, offering visitors an authentic taste of Sardinia's land, sea, and wild landscapes. Whether enjoying a robust glass of Cannonau with a plate of roasted Porceddu, sipping a chilled glass of Vermentino alongside a seafood feast, or finishing a meal with a smooth shot of Mirto, these traditional beverages offer an unforgettable experience of Sardinian flavors and craftsmanship. These drinks can be found in vineyards, enotecas, traditional restaurants, and specialty shops across the island, making it easy for visitors to explore, taste, and bring home a piece of Sardinia's rich wine and spirit culture. Whether visiting a family-run cantina in the countryside, sampling rare vintages in an elegant seaside wine bar, or enjoying a homemade Mirto after a traditional Sardinian meal, these local beverages offer a deep connection to the island's history, people, and passion for high-quality craftsmanship, making them an essential part of any trip to Sardinia.

Exploring Local Markets

Sardinia is home to a vibrant network of local markets, where visitors can experience the island's rich traditions, fresh produce, artisanal crafts, and authentic culinary delights. These markets are the heart of Sardinian culture, offering a glimpse into the daily lives of locals, the island's agricultural abundance, and its deep-rooted connection to handmade goods and time-honored recipes. Whether located in historic city centers, coastal towns, or rural villages, these markets provide a unique opportunity to sample fresh Sardinian cheeses, taste locally produced honey, buy handcrafted ceramics, and pick up some of the island's finest cured meats, olives, and wines. Some markets operate daily, while others take place only once or twice a week, making them special events where visitors can interact with farmers, artisans, and vendors. Shopping at local markets is also an affordable way to experience Sardinian gastronomy, as many products are cheaper than in supermarkets and gourmet stores while maintaining superior quality.

One of the most famous and historically significant markets in Sardinia is San Benedetto Market (Mercato di San Benedetto) in Cagliari, widely regarded as one of the largest indoor markets in Italy and the best place to explore the island's diverse food culture. Located in the heart of Cagliari, just a short walk from the city center, this two-level market is a paradise for food lovers, offering an impressive selection of fresh seafood, locally produced cheeses, seasonal fruits and vegetables, meats, bread, olive oil, and traditional Sardinian sweets. The market is particularly famous for its seafood section, where local fishermen sell their daily catch, including swordfish, red tuna, octopus, mussels, and prawns, all freshly caught from the Mediterranean. The upstairs section is dedicated to meats, cheeses, and baked goods, where visitors can find Pecorino Sardo, Bottarga (cured mullet roe), Pane Carasau (traditional crispy flatbread), and artisanal honey. Vendors also sell homemade Mirto liqueur, extra virgin olive oil, and hand-rolled pasta, including the famous Fregola. The market operates Monday to Saturday from 7:00 AM to 2:00 PM, and prices are very reasonable compared to high-end specialty stores, with fresh fish costing around €10 to €25 per kilogram, cheeses ranging from €8 to €20 per kilogram, and Sardinian bread available for as little as €2 per loaf. Visitors arriving from Cagliari's central train station can reach the market by walking for 15 minutes or taking bus routes 1 and M, which stop directly near the entrance. This market is a must-visit for food enthusiasts, offering an authentic and immersive experience of Sardinia's culinary traditions.

Another must-visit market is the Alghero Weekly Market (Mercato di Alghero), held every Wednesday morning in Piazzale della Pace, just a short walk from Alghero's old town and seafront promenade. This bustling outdoor market is one of the largest in northern Sardinia, featuring a wide variety of local produce, fresh seafood, handmade crafts, and traditional Sardinian textiles. The market is best known for its selection of locally made cheeses and cured meats, with vendors selling fresh Ricotta, Pecorino Fiore Sardo, Salame Sardo, and Prosciutto di Villagrande, all produced in the nearby hills of the Sassari and Barbagia regions. Shoppers can also browse through handwoven baskets, ceramics, traditional Sardinian jewelry, and embroidered textiles, making it an excellent place to find unique souvenirs and gifts. Prices are affordable, with cheese starting at €10 per kilogram, handmade baskets costing around €15 to €40, and locally produced liqueurs available for €10 to €25 per bottle. The best way to reach the market is by walking from Alghero's city center or taking a local bus to Piazzale della Pace. This market is an ideal stop for those looking to experience the vibrant atmosphere of a traditional Sardinian street market while enjoying spectacular views of Alghero's coastline.

For those looking to experience a true farmer's market atmosphere, the Oristano Farmers' Market (Mercato di Campagna Amica Oristano) is a fantastic choice. Located in Piazza Eleonora d'Arborea, this weekly Saturday morning market is one of the best places to buy farm-fresh produce directly from local farmers. The market specializes in seasonal fruits and vegetables, organic honey, artisanal bread, homemade jams, and farm-raised meats, all produced by small-scale Sardinian farmers and rural cooperatives. The market is particularly known for its freshly harvested artichokes, tomatoes, oranges, almonds, and wild herbs, making it an excellent spot to pick up organic and sustainable products at fair prices. Honey lovers will find some of the finest Sardinian varieties, including asphodel, eucalyptus, and thistle honey, priced between €6 and €12 per jar, while fresh vegetables and fruits typically cost €2 to €4 per kilogram. Visitors can also find freshly baked Sardinian pastries, such as Sebadas (honey-drizzled cheese pastries) and Amaretti cookies, alongside bottles of local Cannonau and Vermentino wine. The market is easily accessible by foot from Oristano's city center, with ample parking available nearby for those arriving by car. This market is ideal for those who want to support local farmers and purchase high-quality organic products straight from the source.

In the northern part of the island, the Sassari Central Market (Mercato Civico di Sassari) is another fantastic option for visitors looking to explore Sardinia's rich food culture. Located in Piazza Mercato, this historic covered market offers a diverse selection of local delicacies, including cheeses, fresh seafood, meats, bread, and spices. The market has a lively and authentic atmosphere, where vendors passionately sell handmade Pecorino cheese, artisanal sausages, wild-foraged mushrooms, sun-dried tomatoes, and local olive oil. It is also a great place to buy dried herbs and spices, including Sardinian saffron and wild fennel, which are commonly used in traditional island recipes. The market operates Monday to Saturday from 7:30 AM to 1:30 PM, with prices that are generally cheaper than supermarkets, offering excellent value for visitors looking to bring home authentic Sardinian ingredients. The best way to reach the market is by walking from Sassari's historic center or taking a local bus to Piazza Mercato. This market is a hidden gem for food lovers, offering a glimpse into the daily life of Sardinian residents while providing access to some of the freshest local products available.

For those visiting the northeastern coast, the Olbia Weekly Market (Mercato di Olbia), held every Tuesday morning in Via Sangallo, is an excellent place to explore local Sardinian specialties. This large open-air market features vendors selling fresh seafood, seasonal fruits, cheeses, and handmade crafts, making it a popular spot for both locals and tourists. The market is best known for its selection of freshly caught seafood, including octopus, sea bass, and anchovies, as well as its variety of Sardinian wines and olive oils. Many vendors also sell handcrafted leather goods, ceramics, and coral jewelry, making it a great place to pick up authentic Sardinian souvenirs. Prices are reasonable, with fresh seafood costing around €10 to €20 per kilogram, handcrafted ceramics starting at €10, and bottles of high-quality olive oil available for €8 to €15. The market is located just a 10-minute walk from Olbia's historic center, with easy access via public buses or taxis from Olbia Costa Smeralda Airport. This market is an excellent place to experience the lively energy of Sardinia's market culture while shopping for fresh, high-quality goods at fair prices.

Visiting Sardinia's best local markets provides an authentic and immersive experience, allowing travelers to discover the island's culinary delights, meet local artisans, and take home high-quality Sardinian products. Whether in Cagliari, Alghero, Oristano, Sassari, or Olbia, these markets offer a rich selection of fresh produce, seafood, cheeses, wines, and handmade crafts, making them an essential stop for anyone looking to experience the true essence of Sardinian culture.

CHAPTER 7: OUTDOOR ADVENTURES

Hiking & Trekking

Sardinia is a hiker's paradise, offering a diverse landscape that ranges from rugged mountains and deep canyons to coastal cliffs and lush forests, making it one of the best destinations in the Mediterranean for trekking and outdoor adventures. Whether you are an experienced trekker seeking challenging climbs or a casual walker looking for scenic trails with breathtaking views, Sardinia has something for everyone. The island's unique geological formations, rich biodiversity, and ancient ruins provide a stunning backdrop for exploration. Many hiking routes pass through national parks, UNESCO-listed sites, and remote wilderness areas, allowing visitors to experience unspoiled nature, rare wildlife, and Sardinian history firsthand. Most of these trails are free to access, though some require guided tours, permits, or entrance fees for conservation purposes. Equipment such as hiking boots, trekking poles, and GPS devices can be rented from outdoor activity centers in major towns and near popular hiking areas. Age restrictions vary depending on the difficulty of the route, with some challenging treks recommended only for experienced hikers, while others are suitable for families and beginners.

One of the most famous and awe-inspiring hiking routes in Sardinia is the Gorropu Canyon Trail, leading to Gola di

Gorropu, often referred to as "Europe's Grand Canyon". This deep limestone gorge, with towering cliffs reaching up to 500 meters high, is one of the deepest canyons in Europe and offers an unforgettable adventure for nature lovers and experienced trekkers. Located in the Supramonte mountain range in eastern Sardinia, the most common starting point for the hike is Genna Silana Pass, which can be reached via the SS125 scenic road from Cala Gonone or Dorgali. The round-trip hike from Genna Silana takes approximately 5-6 hours, covering rocky terrain with steep descents and uneven paths, making it suitable for experienced hikers with proper footwear and navigation skills. Alternatively, a shorter and less strenuous route begins near the Flumineddu River, where visitors can follow a flatter 2-hour trail along the riverbed before reaching the gorge. There is a €5 to €10 entrance fee for visitors wishing to explore the interior of the canyon, and guided tours are available for those who want to learn more about the geology, wildlife, and history of this spectacular natural wonder. Hiking equipment, including helmets, sturdy shoes, and trekking poles, can be rented from outdoor centers in Cala Gonone, Dorgali, and Baunei for around €10 to €25 per day. The trail is not recommended for young children or those with mobility issues, as the rocky sections require careful navigation.

For those seeking coastal scenery and panoramic sea views, the Selvaggio Blu Trek is considered one of the most challenging and rewarding treks in Italy. This multi-day adventure follows the rugged cliffs of the Gulf of Orosei, offering dramatic sea views, hidden coves, and limestone caves, making it a dream route for experienced hikers and climbers. The trail begins in Santa Maria Navarrese, a small coastal town in eastern Sardinia, and stretches for over 40 kilometers along the unspoiled coastline. The trek takes 4 to 6 days to complete, passing through remote beaches such as Cala Goloritzé, Cala Sisine, and Cala Mariolu, where hikers can swim in crystal-clear waters before continuing the journey. Due to its extreme difficulty, involving steep ascents, technical scrambling, and sections requiring ropes, this trek is recommended only for highly experienced hikers or those accompanied by professional guides. Guided tours with logistical support, overnight camping, and food provisions are available for around €700 to €1,200 per person, depending on the package and duration. Equipment such as harnesses, helmets, and climbing ropes can be rented in Baunei and Santa Maria Navarrese, with daily rental costs ranging from €15 to €50. This trek is not suitable for children or beginners, as sections involve dangerous cliffs and high levels of endurance. However, for those with the necessary skills and stamina, it is considered one of the most rewarding hiking experiences in Sardinia.

For a family-friendly and scenic hike, the Sella del Diavolo Trail in Cagliari offers a relatively easy trek with stunning coastal views. Located just a few kilometers from Cagliari's city center, this short 2-hour loop trail leads to the top of the Sella del Diavolo (Devil's Saddle), a prominent limestone promontory overlooking Poetto Beach and the Gulf of Angels. The trail begins at Calamosca Beach, where visitors can park their cars or arrive by public bus from Cagliari's central station. The hike follows a gentle incline, passing through Mediterranean vegetation, ancient military ruins, and limestone cliffs, before reaching a spectacular viewpoint at the summit. From here, hikers can enjoy panoramic views of Cagliari's coastline, the salt flats of Molentargius Nature Park, and the distant mountains of southern Sardinia. The hike is free of charge, requires no special equipment beyond comfortable shoes and sun protection, and is suitable for all ages, making it a perfect outdoor activity for families, casual hikers, and photography enthusiasts.

For those interested in archaeological hiking routes, the Monte Tiscali Hike in central Sardinia offers a unique combination of nature, history, and adventure. The trail leads to Tiscali, an ancient Nuragic village hidden inside a collapsed limestone sinkhole, believed to have been inhabited over 3,000 years ago. Located in the Supramonte region near Dorgali and Oliena, the round-trip hike to Tiscali takes about 3-4 hours, with moderate difficulty involving rocky terrain and short but steep climbs. The trail begins at Valle di Lanaitto, accessible by car from Dorgali via the SS129 and SP38 roads, followed by a short dirt track leading to the parking area. Upon reaching the Tiscali archaeological site, visitors can explore the remains of ancient stone dwellings while enjoying breathtaking views of the surrounding mountains and valleys. There is a €5 to €10 entrance fee to access the site, with optional guided tours available to explain the history and significance of the Nuragic civilization. Basic hiking gear, including sturdy shoes, water bottles, and trekking poles, can be rented from outdoor shops in Dorgali and Oliena, with prices ranging from €8 to €20 per day. This hike is suitable for families with older children (ages 8 and up) and history enthusiasts, offering a fascinating journey through Sardinia's prehistoric past in a stunning natural setting.

For those looking to explore forested landscapes and wildlife, the Monte Arcosu Nature Reserve near Cagliari offers a variety of well-marked trails through protected woodlands, home to rare Sardinian deer, wild boars, and golden eagles. The reserve is part of the WWF conservation area, providing an eco-friendly hiking experience with trails ranging from easy nature walks to challenging summit climbs. Located about 25 kilometers west of Cagliari, Monte Arcosu can be reached by car via the SS195 road towards Capoterra, with parking available near the reserve's entrance. The trails are open year-round, with a small entrance fee of €5 to €10 per person to support conservation efforts. Equipment is not required for most trails, but binoculars, hiking boots, and water bottles are recommended for those planning to spend several hours in the reserve's dense oak forests and scenic viewpoints. This hike is ideal for nature lovers, families, and birdwatchers, providing a peaceful escape into Sardinia's natural beauty.

With its diverse landscapes, historical sites, and breathtaking coastal paths, Sardinia offers some of the best hiking and trekking routes in the Mediterranean, catering to all levels of experience, from casual walkers to expert climbers. Whether exploring ancient ruins, deep canyons, panoramic sea cliffs, or lush forests, each hike offers a unique adventure into the heart of Sardinia's natural and cultural wonders.

Water Sports & Coastal Activities

With its strong Mediterranean winds, hidden coves, and rich marine biodiversity, the island is a top location for kitesurfing, windsurfing, scuba diving, snorkeling, sailing, kayaking, and stand-up paddleboarding (SUP). Whether visitors prefer riding the waves, exploring underwater caves, or paddling along scenic coastlines, Sardinia's varied seascapes provide an ideal setting. Many of these activities are available year-round, with the peak season running from May to October when the waters are warmest and conditions are optimal. Equipment rental shops, guided tours, and professional instructors are available in major coastal towns and popular tourist areas, ensuring that both beginners and experienced adventurers can safely enjoy the island's water-based activities. Prices vary depending on the activity, duration, and whether guided services are included, and some sports may have age restrictions for safety reasons.

One of the most popular water sports in Sardinia is kitesurfing, which is best enjoyed in Porto Pollo, near Palau, and Punta Trettu in the southwest near Sant'Antioco. These spots are famous for their steady winds, shallow waters, and wide-open beaches, making them perfect for both beginners and advanced riders. Porto Pollo is particularly renowned among the international kitesurfing community, attracting visitors from all over the world due to its consistent wind conditions created by the natural wind corridor between Sardinia and Corsica. Several kitesurfing schools and rental centers operate in the area, including Porto Pollo Kite School and Kite Sardegna, offering lessons for all skill levels. Equipment rental for a full day costs around €50 to €90, while beginner lessons, which include equipment and instructor guidance, range from €100 to €150 per session. Punta Trettu, on the other hand, offers flat, shallow waters, making it an excellent location for beginners learning to kitesurf in a safe and controlled environment. Lessons are available for both individual and group sessions, with courses lasting from a single day to full week-long training programs. Due to the strong winds and physical demands, kitesurfing is generally recommended for ages 12 and up, with younger children requiring parental supervision and specialized beginner courses.

For those who prefer windsurfing, Sardinia offers several world-class windsurfing locations, including Porto Pollo, Chia, and Poetto Beach in Cagliari. Windsurfing conditions vary depending on the season, with stronger mistral winds between autumn and spring, and gentler breezes in the summer months. Porto Pollo remains one of the most popular spots, offering ideal conditions for freestyle and wave windsurfing, while Chia, located on the southern coast near Domus de Maria, is perfect for those seeking a mix of waves and flat-water sailing. Poetto Beach, just minutes from Cagliari's city center, is an excellent place for beginners, with plenty of rental shops and instructors available. Windsurfing equipment rental ranges from €40 to €80 per day, while lessons start at €70 per session. Most schools offer beginner-friendly courses, and children as young as 8 years old can start learning under the guidance of professional instructors.

Scuba diving is another must-try water activity in Sardinia, thanks to the island's crystal-clear waters, vibrant marine life, and fascinating underwater caves. Some of the best diving spots include the Marine Protected Area of Tavolara and Punta Coda Cavallo, Capo Carbonara near Villasimius, and the stunning Grotta del Nereo near Alghero, which is one of the largest underwater caves in the Mediterranean. These sites are home to colorful coral reefs, barracudas, groupers, and even occasional dolphins and sea turtles. Certified diving centers such as Tavolara Diving Center, Pro Dive Sardinia, and Diving Alghero offer guided dives, introductory courses, and certification programs. A single guided dive costs between €50 and €90, while PADI certification courses start at €400 for beginners. Equipment rental is available at all major dive centers, typically costing €25 to €40 per day for a full diving kit. Most dive sites require participants to be at least 10 years old for introductory dives, while advanced dives in caves and deep-water locations are restricted to certified divers with prior experience.

For visitors who prefer a less technical but equally breathtaking underwater experience, snorkeling is an excellent option. Sardinia's coastline offers numerous snorkeling-friendly locations with shallow reefs, hidden coves, and marine reserves teeming with life. Some of the best snorkeling spots include Cala Goloritzé, La Maddalena Archipelago, Cala Mariolu, and Capo Testa, where visitors can explore rock formations, underwater caves, and schools of vibrant fish. Snorkeling gear, including masks, snorkels, and fins, can be rented from beachside kiosks and dive centers for around €10 to €20 per day. Many guided snorkeling tours are available, often combined with boat excursions, costing between €35 and €70 per person. Snorkeling is a family-friendly activity, with no strict age restrictions, although children should always be supervised by an adult when exploring deeper waters.

Sailing is another fantastic way to experience Sardinia's coastline, offering a mix of relaxation and adventure while exploring hidden beaches, sea caves, and secluded islands. The La Maddalena Archipelago, Costa Smeralda, and the Gulf of Orosei are some of the most popular areas for sailing excursions. Visitors can rent private sailboats, join guided sailing tours, or take sailing lessons at locations such as Porto Cervo, Palau, and Villasimius. Half-day and full-day sailing trips range from €80 to €200 per person, with private charters costing between €500 and €1,500 per day, depending on the size of the boat and additional services included. Many of these excursions feature stops at uninhabited islands, swimming breaks, and onboard meals featuring local Sardinian cuisine. No prior experience is necessary for joining a guided sailing trip, but those interested in learning how to sail can take lessons at local sailing schools, where courses range from €150 to €500 depending on the duration and level of instruction.

For those looking for a more peaceful and accessible water activity, kayaking and stand-up paddleboarding (SUP) are fantastic ways to explore Sardinia's stunning coastline at a relaxed pace. The best locations for kayaking and SUP include Cala Luna, Capo Caccia, and the Gulf of Orosei, where visitors can paddle along sea cliffs, through natural rock arches, and into hidden caves. Kayak and SUP rentals are available at beach resorts, water sports centers, and tour operators, with rental prices ranging from €15 to €40 per hour, depending on the location and equipment type. Guided kayak tours, which often include stops for snorkeling and swimming, cost between €50 and €100 per person. These activities are suitable for all ages, with lightweight kayaks and paddleboards available for children and beginners.

Sardinia's breathtaking coastline, favorable wind conditions, and rich marine biodiversity make it an ideal destination for water sports enthusiasts of all skill levels. Whether visitors want to experience the thrill of kitesurfing and windsurfing, explore the underwater world through diving and snorkeling, or enjoy a leisurely day sailing or kayaking, Sardinia offers an abundance of opportunities to connect with the sea and enjoy the island's natural beauty in a thrilling and unforgettable way.

Climbing & Caving

The island's diverse geological formations make it an ideal playground for climbers and spelunkers of all skill levels, whether they seek technical ascents on dramatic coastal crags or mysterious underground adventures in prehistoric caves. The island's mild climate allows for climbing and caving year-round, although the best seasons are spring and autumn when temperatures are comfortable. Most climbing areas and caves are located in natural parks or remote regions, meaning hiring a guide or joining a tour is often the best way to access these hidden gems. Equipment rental is available in specialized outdoor shops and climbing centers in major towns such as Nuoro, Dorgali, and Alghero, with costs varying based on the activity and duration. While some climbing and caving routes are suitable for families and beginners, others require advanced skills, technical equipment, and professional guidance.

For rock climbers, Cala Gonone on the east coast of Sardinia is a world-renowned climbing destination, offering hundreds of bolted routes on limestone cliffs with breathtaking views of the Gulf of Orosei. The area is famous for its sport climbing routes, ranging from easy grades for beginners to extreme overhangs for advanced climbers. Some of the most famous climbing crags in Cala Gonone include Biddiriscottai, La Poltrona, and Cala Fuili, each offering a unique mix of vertical walls, technical slabs, and tufas. The routes are well-maintained, with stainless steel bolts and anchors, making it a safe and enjoyable climbing experience. Climbers can reach Cala Gonone by car from Olbia or Cagliari via the SS125 scenic coastal road, or by taking a bus from Nuoro. Equipment rental is available at climbing shops in Cala Gonone, with costs for harnesses, ropes, and climbing shoes ranging from €10 to €30 per day. Guided climbing excursions are also available, with half-day sessions costing around €50 to €100 per person, depending on the route difficulty and group size. There are no strict age restrictions, but beginners and younger climbers should book a guided session to ensure safety.

For those looking for adventurous multi-pitch climbing, Supramonte, located in central Sardinia, offers some of the most demanding and rewarding climbing routes on the island. The massive limestone walls of Monte Oddeu and Punta Cusidore provide climbers with routes ranging from long traditional climbs to difficult sport climbs, attracting expert climbers from around the world. The region also features deep gorges and caves, making it a great spot for combining climbing and caving in a single adventure. The best way to access Supramonte is by driving from Dorgali or Oliena, with well-marked trails leading to the base of the climbing walls. Due to the remote nature of these routes, it is recommended to hire a local guide, especially for first-time visitors. Guided tours for multi-pitch climbing cost between €80 and €150 per person, including safety gear and expert instruction. Climbers should bring their own equipment, though rope, helmets, and belay devices can be rented for around €20 to €40 per day. Most routes in Supramonte are recommended for experienced climbers, though there are some easier routes for intermediate-level climbers.

For a unique deepwater soloing experience, Capo Caccia near Alghero offers dramatic sea cliffs that can be climbed without ropes, with the safety of the sea below. This is a thrilling style of climbing where climbers ascend overhanging walls directly above deep water, allowing them to fall safely into the sea if they lose their grip. Some of the best spots include Grotta dei Vasi Rotti and Cala

Dragunara, where climbers can enjoy overhanging limestone cliffs rising directly from the turquoise sea. To reach Capo Caccia, visitors can take a boat from Alghero's marina or drive along the SP55 scenic coastal road. Since deepwater soloing requires confidence in both climbing and swimming, it is best suited for advanced climbers, though beginners can book a guided deepwater soloing session for around €70 to €120 per person. Equipment such as climbing shoes and chalk bags can be rented from climbing centers in Alghero. There are no strict age restrictions, but participants should be strong swimmers and comfortable with falling into open water.

For those interested in underground exploration, Sardinia is home to some of the most impressive caves in Europe, many of which offer guided caving tours for visitors of all skill levels. One of the most famous caves is Grotta di Nettuno (Neptune's Grotto), located in Capo Caccia near Alghero, a spectacular sea cave featuring massive stalactites, underground lakes, and dramatic rock formations. The cave can be reached by taking a boat from Alghero's marina or by descending the Escala del Cabirol, a staircase of 654 steps carved into the cliffside. The entrance fee for the guided tour inside the cave is around €14 per adult and €10 per child, with tours available year-round. No special equipment is needed, as walkways and handrails are in place, making it accessible for families and children.

For a more extreme caving experience, Grotta del Bue Marino, located near Cala Gonone, is an incredible underground system featuring long tunnels, underground rivers, and prehistoric cave paintings. Named after the monk seal (Bue Marino) that once inhabited the cave, this site is accessible only by boat from Cala Gonone or via a long hike from Cala Fuili. Visitors can choose between a basic guided tour of the main chamber for around €15 per person or a more advanced speleological tour, which requires helmets, headlamps, and climbing harnesses. The more technical caving tours cost between €50 and €100 per person and are recommended for visitors aged 12 and up due to the physical challenges involved.

For those seeking one of the most technical cave adventures in Sardinia, Su Bentu and Sa Oche Cave System near Oliena and Supramonte is considered one of the longest cave networks in Italy, stretching over 18 kilometers underground. This cave features underground waterfalls, deep tunnels, and narrow passageways, making it ideal for experienced cavers with advanced skills. Guided caving expeditions range from €80 to €200 per person, depending on the length and difficulty of the route. Due to the extreme nature of this cave, participants must be at least 16 years old, and full caving gear, including helmets, harnesses, wetsuits, and headlamps, is required. Equipment can be rented from caving and adventure tour operators in Oliena and Dorgali, with full gear rental costing around €30 to €50 per day.

Sardinia's rock climbing and caving opportunities provide an unforgettable mix of adventure, natural beauty, and technical challenges, catering to both casual explorers and seasoned professionals. Whether scaling limestone cliffs overlooking the sea, venturing deep into ancient underground caves, or testing your skills on world-class multi-pitch routes, the island offers some of the most exciting climbing and caving experiences in Europe. With expert guides, rental equipment, and well-developed routes available across the island, visitors can safely enjoy Sardinia's thrilling landscapes while experiencing the raw, untamed beauty of its mountains and caves.

Wildlife Encounters

Sardinia is a paradise for wildlife enthusiasts, offering an incredible variety of habitats that support unique and diverse species found nowhere else in the world. From coastal wetlands teeming with flamingos to rugged mountain ranges where wild boars and Sardinian deer roam, and crystal-clear waters where dolphins and monk seals can sometimes be spotted, the island provides countless opportunities for wildlife watching. Whether exploring protected national parks, marine reserves, or remote forested areas, visitors can observe rare species in their natural habitats while enjoying Sardinia's breathtaking landscapes. The best time for wildlife watching is typically spring and autumn, when temperatures are mild, and animal activity is at its peak. Many wildlife-rich areas can be visited for free or at a small entry fee, while guided tours with expert naturalists are available for a more immersive and educational experience. Some excursions require binoculars, spotting scopes, and cameras, which can be rented from local tour operators and visitor centers. Age restrictions vary depending on the location and activity, with some wildlife tours suitable for families and children, while others require hiking experience and endurance.

One of the best places for birdwatching in Sardinia is Molentargius-Saline Regional Park, located near Cagliari. This vast wetland and salt marsh ecosystem is home to thousands of pink flamingos, herons, egrets, and many migratory birds that nest in the park throughout the year. The flamingos are particularly stunning in spring and summer, when their bright pink feathers create a striking contrast against the turquoise waters. The park is accessible by public bus from Cagliari's city center or by bike along scenic cycling paths from Poetto Beach. Entrance to the park is free, but visitors can rent bicycles for €10 to €20 per day or book guided wildlife tours for around €30 per person, which include expert insights into the area's bird species, salt harvesting traditions, and wetland conservation efforts. The park has well-marked trails and observation platforms, making it suitable for all ages, and families with children can enjoy interactive educational activities at the visitor center.

For those interested in mammal watching, Monte Arcosu Nature Reserve, located about 25 kilometers from Cagliari, is a must-visit destination. This vast protected forest, managed by the World Wildlife Fund (WWF), is one of the best places to see the elusive Sardinian deer, wild boars, and golden eagles in their natural habitat. The reserve is also home to mouflons (wild sheep), foxes, and rare birds of prey, including peregrine falcons and griffon vultures. To reach the reserve, visitors can drive from Cagliari along the SS195 road towards Capoterra, where there is a designated parking area near the entrance. Entry fees are €5 to €10 per person, which support conservation projects. Guided tours and wildlife photography workshops are available for €30 to €50 per person, providing opportunities to observe animals at dawn and dusk when they are most active. The reserve has a network of hiking trails, ranging from easy walks to challenging treks, and binoculars and spotting scopes can be rented for around €10 per day. The trails are family-friendly, and children over six years old can participate in guided wildlife tours.

For marine wildlife enthusiasts, the Asinara National Park in northern Sardinia offers an unforgettable experience. Asinara Island is one of the most untouched and protected areas in the Mediterranean, known for its albino donkeys, wild goats, peregrine falcons, and monk seals, as well as its thriving marine ecosystem. The island can be accessed by ferry from Porto Torres or Stintino, with boats departing regularly throughout the day. Once on the island, visitors can explore by foot, bicycle, or electric jeep, all of which are available for rent at the park entrance. The albino donkeys, unique to Asinara, are among the most fascinating sights, along with Corsican gulls, cormorants, and dolphins that often swim near the coast. Entry to the park is free, but ferry tickets cost €15 to €25 per person, and guided safaris cost between €40 and €80 per person, depending on the tour package. Snorkeling and diving tours in the protected marine area are available for those who want to observe sea turtles, rays, and colorful fish species, with rental equipment available for €20 to €40 per session. Since Asinara is a protected area, visitor numbers are regulated, and it is recommended to book guided tours in advance, especially during the summer months.

For visitors who want to explore Sardinia's mountainous interior and its diverse wildlife, the Gennargentu National Park is an excellent choice. This remote and rugged region, located in the heart of Sardinia, is home to rare species such as the Sardinian wildcat, golden eagles, and European mouflons, as well as some of the island's oldest forests and highest peaks. The best access points to the park are from Fonni or Desulo, where local tour operators offer guided wildlife treks for around €50 to €100 per person, depending on the length and difficulty of the hike. One of the most popular routes leads to Punta La Marmora, Sardinia's highest peak at 1,834 meters, where hikers can enjoy breathtaking views over the island while spotting eagles soaring overhead. The area is also known for its wild horses, which can often be seen grazing in the meadows near Lake Gusana. Due to the remote and rugged terrain, it is recommended to bring sturdy hiking boots, warm clothing, and binoculars. Many local guides offer wildlife tracking tours, where visitors can learn how to identify animal footprints, bird calls, and natural shelters used by Sardinia's native species. The park is suitable for adults and children over eight years old, though some steep trails may be challenging for younger hikers.

For a unique and off-the-beaten-path wildlife experience, the Giara di Gesturi Plateau offers an opportunity to see the famous Cavallini della Giara, a breed of small wild horses that have roamed Sardinia for centuries. This protected natural area, located in central Sardinia near Barumini, is a flat, volcanic plateau covered in oak forests, wildflowers, and seasonal lakes, where the horses roam freely alongside hedgehogs, foxes, and hoopoe birds. Visitors can explore the plateau via marked hiking trails, or book a guided horseback riding tour for €30 to €60 per person, allowing them to observe the wild horses up close without disturbing them. The best way to reach Giara di Gesturi is by driving from Cagliari or Oristano via the SS197 road, with parking available near the Giara Nature Center. The wild horses are best seen in the early morning or late afternoon, and visitors should bring binoculars and cameras to capture their movements in the vast, open landscape. This wildlife-watching experience is suitable for all ages, making it a great option for families and nature lovers looking for a peaceful and immersive adventure.

With its rich biodiversity, diverse landscapes, and protected nature reserves, Sardinia offers some of the best wildlife-watching opportunities in Europe, catering to both casual nature lovers and dedicated wildlife enthusiasts. Whether spotting flamingos in coastal wetlands, tracking rare mammals in the mountains, or observing marine life in crystal-clear waters, visitors can enjoy an unforgettable experience connecting with Sardinia's unique and unspoiled natural world. Many wildlife tours and excursions offer expert guidance, rental equipment, and eco-friendly experiences, ensuring that visitors can appreciate the island's fauna while contributing to conservation efforts.

CONCLUSION: PRACTICAL TIPS & TRAVEL ITINERARIES

Money Matters: Currency, Banking & Budgeting

Sardinia, like the rest of Italy, uses the Euro (€) as its official currency, and visitors should be well-prepared when it comes to managing their money, banking needs, and overall travel budget. While Sardinia is generally more affordable than mainland Italy, especially compared to major cities like Rome and Milan, costs can vary significantly depending on the season, location, and type of activities planned. Understanding how to handle currency exchange, banking services, and budgeting strategies will help visitors make the most of their trip while avoiding unnecessary expenses and financial inconveniences.

For those arriving from outside the Eurozone, exchanging currency before traveling or upon arrival at banks, currency exchange offices, or ATMs is recommended. While some exchange offices are available at major airports like Cagliari Elmas, Olbia Costa Smeralda, and Alghero-Fertilia, they often charge higher commission fees compared to banks and ATMs. Banks in Sardinia, such as Intesa Sanpaolo, UniCredit, Banco di Sardegna, and BPER Banca, offer currency exchange services at competitive rates, though many require a passport for identification when exchanging money. Banks are generally open Monday to Friday from 8:30 AM to 1:30 PM, with a shorter afternoon session from 2:30 PM to 4:00 PM, and they are closed on weekends and public holidays. For those needing cash outside of banking hours, ATMs, locally known as "Bancomat", are widely available in cities, towns, and even some rural areas.

Using ATMs is the most convenient way to withdraw Euros, as they typically offer the best exchange rates with lower fees compared to currency exchange offices. However, withdrawal fees vary depending on the visitor's bank, with some international banks charging a flat fee of €3 to €6 per transaction plus an additional percentage-based fee. To minimize fees, travelers should consider using bank accounts or credit cards that offer free foreign ATM withdrawals. ATMs in Sardinia accept major international cards, including Visa, Mastercard, Maestro, and Cirrus, though some smaller ATMs may not support American Express. It is advisable to inform one's bank before traveling to avoid unexpected transaction blocks due to foreign activity.

Credit and debit cards are widely accepted in hotels, restaurants, and larger stores, but smaller businesses, street vendors, and rural establishments may only accept cash. Contactless payment methods such as Apple Pay, Google Pay, and Samsung Pay are becoming increasingly popular in major cities and tourist areas, but travelers should always carry some cash, especially when visiting remote villages, outdoor markets, or traditional trattorias. Tipping is not mandatory in Sardinia, as service charges are often included in restaurant bills, but leaving a small amount of change or rounding up the bill is appreciated for good service.

Budgeting for a trip to Sardinia depends on several factors, including accommodation choices, transportation, dining preferences, and activities. On average, a budget traveler can expect to spend around €50 to €80 per day, staying in hostels or budget hotels, using public transportation, and eating at local trattorias or markets. A mid-range traveler looking for more comfortable accommodations, occasional dining at sit-down restaurants, and a mix of paid excursions and activities should budget around €100 to €200 per day. Those opting for luxury hotels, private tours, fine dining, and premium experiences can expect to spend €250 or more per day.

Accommodation costs vary depending on the season and location. Budget-friendly options such as hostels, guesthouses, and agriturismi (farm stays) range from €30 to €80 per night, while mid-range hotels and boutique accommodations typically cost €100 to €200 per night. Luxury hotels and resorts, especially in Costa Smeralda and high-end coastal areas, can charge €300 or more per night, particularly during the peak summer months of July and August.

Food expenses can be kept low by dining at local markets, bakeries, and pizzerias, where meals cost between €5 and €15. Traditional Sardinian cuisine is hearty and affordable, and many local trattorias offer set menus or "menu del giorno" (daily specials) for around €15 to €25, including a starter, main course, and wine. Fine dining experiences, especially at seaside seafood restaurants, typically cost €40 to €80 per person, with higher-end restaurants in luxury areas like Porto Cervo charging even more.

Transportation costs also vary depending on whether visitors rent a car, use public transport, or take guided tours. Renting a car is one of the best ways to explore Sardinia, particularly for those wanting to visit remote beaches, national parks, and small inland villages. Car rental prices start at €30 to €70 per day, depending on the vehicle type, season, and insurance coverage. Fuel prices are relatively high, averaging around €1.80 to €2.10 per liter, making long-distance driving an added expense to consider when budgeting. For those relying on public transportation, bus fares within cities cost around €1.30 per ride, while regional bus routes range from €5 to €20, depending on the distance. Train travel is limited but affordable, with routes connecting major cities like Cagliari, Sassari, Oristano, and Olbia, with ticket prices ranging from €10 to €30, depending on the route.

Activities and excursions can range from free or low-cost nature hikes and beach visits to more expensive guided tours and adventure sports. National parks and historical sites often have entry fees between €5 and €15 per person, while boat tours to La Maddalena Archipelago, Gulf of Orosei, and Asinara National Park cost between €50 and €100 per person, depending on the tour package. Diving, kitesurfing, and guided trekking tours typically range from €50 to €150 per session, while luxury yacht rentals and private experiences can easily exceed €500 per day.

For travelers looking to save money, there are several budget-friendly tips to consider. Traveling during the off-season (late September to early June) can significantly reduce accommodation and flight costs, as prices tend to double or even triple during peak summer months. Booking accommodations in smaller towns or inland areas rather than tourist hotspots can also lead to significant savings. Eating at local markets, bakeries, and casual trattorias rather than upscale restaurants helps keep food expenses low while still enjoying authentic Sardinian cuisine. Using public transportation instead of taxis and taking advantage of multi-day transport passes can help cut down on travel expenses.

Understanding the currency, banking options, and budgeting strategies before visiting Sardinia will allow travelers to manage their finances efficiently and enjoy a stress-free experience. With a mix of affordable options, mid-range comforts, and high-end luxury, visitors can tailor their spending to match their travel style, ensuring they make the most of their time on the island while staying within their preferred budget. Whether choosing a cost-effective backpacking trip, a balanced mid-range itinerary, or a luxurious escape to Sardinia's finest resorts, proper financial planning will enhance the travel experience and allow visitors to focus on the island's stunning landscapes, rich culture, and world-class cuisine without unexpected financial surprises.

One-Week Itinerary

A one-week trip to Sardinia offers the perfect balance of stunning coastal scenery, cultural exploration, outdoor adventures, and gastronomic experiences. The island is vast and diverse, meaning an ideal itinerary should include a mix of its charming cities, breathtaking beaches, historical sites, and unique inland landscapes. Whether visitors are interested in relaxing on the shores of Costa Smeralda, exploring ancient Nuragic ruins, hiking through rugged mountains, or tasting the island's renowned wines and seafood, Sardinia provides a well-rounded travel experience that caters to all types of travelers. Given the size of the island, choosing a well-planned route is essential to make the most of the trip while minimizing unnecessary travel time. Renting a car is highly recommended, as public transportation can be limited in some areas, especially when exploring the more remote regions. The best way to experience Sardinia is to combine the northern and central parts of the island with a touch of the south, allowing visitors to see the most iconic spots while discovering hidden gems along the way.

Starting the journey in Cagliari, Sardinia's capital, is a great way to immerse oneself in the island's culture and history before heading north. Cagliari is rich in historical sites, bustling markets, and a scenic coastline, making it the perfect introduction to Sardinia. Exploring the Castello district, with its medieval streets, Bastione di Saint Remy, and panoramic views over the city, provides a glimpse into the island's past. The San Benedetto Market is a must-visit for those wanting to sample fresh seafood, local cheeses, and traditional Sardinian products. A short drive from the city leads to Poetto Beach, where visitors can relax or take a scenic walk along the coastline. In the afternoon, a visit to Molentargius-Saline Regional Park offers the chance to see pink flamingos in their natural habitat. Dinner in Cagliari should include traditional Sardinian cuisine, with restaurants such as Sa Domu Sarda or Ristorante Antica Cagliari serving dishes like Fregola ai frutti di mare (Sardinian couscous with seafood) and Seadas (honey-drizzled cheese pastries).

On the second day, heading west toward Oristano allows visitors to explore one of Sardinia's most fascinating archaeological sites, Tharros, an ancient Phoenician-Roman city located along the coast. Walking among the ruins of temples, baths, and defensive walls with the sea as a backdrop creates a truly immersive historical experience. Nearby, the Sinis Peninsula is home to some of the most pristine beaches on the island, including Is Arutas, known for its unique quartz sand that resembles grains of rice. Oristano itself is a charming town with narrow streets, traditional bakeries, and elegant piazzas, making it a pleasant stop for a relaxed afternoon stroll. Before continuing the journey, tasting Bottarga (cured fish roe) from Cabras, a local specialty, is a must for food lovers.

Traveling northward on the third day brings visitors to Bosa, one of Sardinia's most picturesque towns, famous for its colorful hillside houses and medieval castle overlooking the Temo River. Walking along the cobblestone streets of Bosa's old town, visiting the Malaspina Castle, and exploring local craft shops provide a charming and authentic experience. A boat trip along the Temo River offers a different perspective of the town, while the nearby Bosa Marina Beach is perfect for a leisurely afternoon swim. Continuing along the coastal road toward Alghero, travelers can stop at Capo Caccia, a dramatic limestone promontory where the famous Neptune's Grotto is located. This vast sea cave, filled with stalactites, underground lakes, and stunning rock formations, is accessible by boat or via the scenic Escala del Cabirol staircase. In Alghero, visitors can enjoy a sunset along the city's historic ramparts, followed by dinner at a seafood restaurant like Al Tuguri or Mabrouk, known for their fresh Catalan-style lobster and grilled fish dishes.

Spending the fourth day in La Maddalena Archipelago is a highlight of any Sardinian itinerary. Taking a ferry from Palau to La Maddalena, visitors can explore crystal-clear waters, hidden coves, and stunning beaches, such as Spiaggia Rosa (Pink Beach) on Budelli Island. Renting a boat or joining a guided excursion allows for stops at some of the most beautiful swimming spots in the Mediterranean, where the turquoise waters rival those of the Caribbean. The town of La Maddalena itself is worth exploring, with its quaint streets, seafood restaurants, and laid-back island atmosphere. Nearby, Caprera Island, once the home of Italian revolutionary Giuseppe Garibaldi, offers both historical sites and scenic hiking trails. Returning to the mainland in the evening, travelers can either stay in Palau or head to Porto Cervo, the heart of the luxurious Costa Smeralda, known for its upscale resorts, designer boutiques, and vibrant nightlife.

On the fifth day, venturing inland toward Supramonte and Gola di Gorropu, one of the deepest canyons in Europe, offers an entirely different perspective of Sardinia's rugged and wild landscapes. This area is a paradise for hikers and nature lovers, with trails leading through dramatic limestone formations, dense forests, and scenic viewpoints. The hike to Gola di Gorropu is a must for adventure seekers, with a challenging but rewarding path leading to towering canyon walls. For those preferring a more relaxed day, the village of Orgosolo, famous for its murals depicting political and social themes, provides a fascinating cultural stop. Traditional shepherd-style lunches, featuring Porceddu (roast suckling pig), Pecorino cheese, and Cannonau wine, can be enjoyed in agriturismi such as Su Gologone, offering an authentic taste of Sardinian mountain cuisine.

On the sixth day, a return to the coast leads to Cala Goloritzé, one of the most iconic beaches in Sardinia, located in the Gulf of Orosei. The beach is accessible by a challenging but breathtaking hike through the Baunei region, taking around 1.5 to 2 hours each way. The effort is well worth it, as visitors arrive at a pristine cove with white pebbles, turquoise waters, and the famous limestone arch rising from the sea. Those who prefer a less strenuous journey can explore the otherworldly beaches of Cala Mariolu and Cala Luna by boat, stopping to swim in sea caves and admire the dramatic coastal cliffs. This day is all about relaxing in nature, swimming in untouched waters, and enjoying Sardinia's unparalleled coastal beauty.

On the final day, making the journey back to Cagliari or Olbia allows time for any last-minute sightseeing, shopping, or culinary indulgences. Those flying out of Cagliari can take the opportunity to visit Poetto Beach once more or explore the city's vibrant markets, while travelers departing from Olbia can enjoy a relaxing morning in the Costa Smeralda region before heading to the airport. Before leaving, picking up local products such as Mirto liqueur, Sardinian ceramics, or handmade textiles makes for great souvenirs to bring home.

This one-week itinerary provides a perfect mix of adventure, relaxation, history, and gastronomy, ensuring visitors experience the best of Sardinia's landscapes, culture, and traditions. Whether exploring ancient ruins, sunbathing on world-class beaches, hiking through rugged mountains, or indulging in local specialties, every day brings a new and unforgettable discovery, making Sardinia a truly unique and enriching travel destination.

Two-Week Itinerary

A two-week itinerary in Sardinia offers the perfect amount of time to explore the island's varied landscapes, rich history, and unique culture. Whether you're traveling for the first time or returning to discover new corners of the island, a well-planned two-week journey will allow you to experience the best of what Sardinia has to offer. From lounging on pristine beaches to hiking through rugged mountains and immersing yourself in the island's fascinating history, this itinerary is designed to provide a balanced and memorable experience.

Day 1–3: Cagliari and the South
Start your adventure in **Cagliari**, the vibrant capital of Sardinia. The city is a wonderful mix of modern life and ancient history. Spend your first day wandering through the **historic district of Castello**, perched high on a hill, offering panoramic views of the surrounding area. Explore **Cagliari's Roman amphitheater**, the **Cathedral of Santa Maria**, and the **National Archaeological Museum**, which houses an impressive collection of artifacts that tell the story of Sardinia's ancient past. Don't miss the **Poetto Beach**, a long stretch of sand just outside the city, perfect for a swim or a stroll at sunset.

On your second day, take a day trip to the **Nora archaeological site**, a fascinating ancient Phoenician and Roman settlement located near Pula, about 30 minutes from Cagliari. The well-preserved ruins, including a Roman theater and thermal baths, offer a glimpse into Sardinia's complex history. Afterward, head to **Capo Spartivento** for a scenic drive along the coast. The region is also known for its charming fishing villages, like **Sant'Antioco**, a lovely spot to explore Sardinia's more remote southern charm.

Day 4–6: Costa Smeralda and the Northeast
From Cagliari, drive north to the world-famous **Costa Smeralda**, one of Sardinia's most luxurious regions. Known for its crystal-clear waters, glamorous resorts, and picturesque villages, Costa Smeralda is an ideal place to unwind and indulge. Spend your time relaxing on the beaches of **Porto Cervo**, **Liscia Ruja**, and **Cala di Volpe**, or take a boat tour to explore the stunning coastline. If you're feeling adventurous, try your hand at water sports such as jet skiing, windsurfing, or diving.

For those interested in Sardinia's history, a visit to **Arzachena's Nuraghe Albucciu** will offer a deep dive into the island's ancient past. You can also visit the **La Maddalena Archipelago**, a group of islands off the coast that boasts some of the most stunning beaches in Sardinia. The ferry ride to **La Maddalena** is scenic and provides an opportunity to enjoy the sea and the islands' unspoiled beauty. On the island, you can hike or simply relax by the crystal-clear waters.

Day 7–9: Olbia and Surroundings
A short drive south from Costa Smeralda, the town of **Olbia** serves as a gateway to many of Sardinia's northern gems. Take the opportunity to explore the town's charming old center, with its **Basilica di San Simplicio** and **archaeological museum**. Afterward, head to the **Basilica di San Simplicio** and the nearby **Isola di Tavolara**, an imposing island known for its rugged cliffs and excellent

hiking opportunities. The island's marine park is great for diving and snorkeling, where you can explore the underwater world of Sardinia's coastline.

The region around Olbia is perfect for those who love the sea, and there are many secluded beaches nearby, such as **Cala Brandinchi**, **Capriccioli**, and **Spiaggia del Principe**, known for their natural beauty. Spend a day exploring these pristine stretches of sand and enjoy the calm, turquoise waters that Sardinia is famous for.

Day 10–12: Oristano and the West Venture west to **Oristano**, a charming town with a rich historical legacy. Explore the **Cathedral of Santa Maria Assunta**, and visit the nearby **Tower of St. Christophoros** and **Tharros**, an ancient Phoenician settlement. Oristano also offers access to some of the most spectacular beaches in Sardinia, including **San Giovanni di Sinis**, **Is Arutas**, and the **Sinis Peninsula**. The latter is home to **Mari Ermi**, a beach made up of fine quartz sand that stretches for miles and offers a serene, untouched atmosphere.

Further inland, you'll find the **Gennargentu Mountains**, perfect for hiking and experiencing Sardinia's rugged natural beauty. The **Gola di Gorropu**, a deep canyon in the mountains, is one of the best places for outdoor adventure. It's a striking location that draws hikers from around the world who come to explore its dramatic cliffs and varied terrain. The mountains also offer beautiful views of the island's unique inland areas, dotted with traditional villages where you can sample local Sardinian cuisine.

Day 13–14: Alghero and the North-West Finish your two-week itinerary in **Alghero**, a beautiful town on the northwest coast of Sardinia that has a distinct Catalan influence. Stroll through the charming **Old Town**, where narrow streets lead to **Piazza Civica**, and visit **the Church of St. Francis** and **the Alghero Cathedral**. Alghero is also known for its coastline, where you can visit **Neptune's Grotto**, an impressive sea cave accessible by boat or a steep staircase.

Spend your last day exploring the **Capo Caccia cliffs**, and if you have time, take a boat trip to the **Asinara National Park**, a protected marine and land reserve known for its pristine beaches, nature, and wildlife. This quiet corner of Sardinia is perfect for a final dose of relaxation before heading home.

This two-week itinerary offers a comprehensive look at Sardinia, blending cultural experiences, natural wonders, historical sites, and plenty of time to relax on the island's stunning beaches. Whether you're hiking through mountains, exploring ancient ruins, or simply lounging by the sea, Sardinia promises an unforgettable journey that will leave you with lasting memories.

Printed in Great Britain
by Amazon